SUBWAY LINE, No. 6

D1549558

Philosophical Thinking is Yoga for the Mind®

"What kind of philosophy would you like instead?"
"The kind that shakes one. That changes one's life."
(J. M. Coetzee)

Upper West Side Philosophers, Inc. provides a
publication venue for original philosophical thinking
steeped in lived life, in line with our motto:
philosophical living & lived philosophy.

YOGA  MIND.

A NEW ETHIC FOR
THINKING AND BEING

MERIDIANS OF THOUGHT

Michael Eskin, Ph.D.
Kathrin Stengel, Ph.D.

New York • Upper West Side Philosophers, Inc.

Published by Upper West Side Philosophers, Inc.
P. O. Box 250645, New York, NY 10025, USA
www.westside-philosophers.com / www.yogaforthemind.us

Meridians of Thought translated from the German by Michael Eskin

In connection with the creation of this book, we would like to thank
Marcelo Guidoli (for helping with the graphics on pp. 73, 80, 82-83,
85, 91-92, 95, 99, 104, and 107), as well as Andrea Boggs (*in memoriam*)
and Licia Carlson.

Library of Congress Cataloging-in-Publication Data

Eskin, Michael.
  Yoga for the mind : a new ethic for thinking and being : meridians of
thought / Michael Eskin, Ph.D., Kathrin Stengel, Ph.D.
      pages cm. -- (Subway line; no. 6)
   ISBN 978-1-935830-09-2 (alk. paper)
  1. Thought and thinking. 2. Yoga--Miscellanea. 3. Philosophy. I.
Stengel, Kathrin. II. Title.
   B105.T54E85 2013
   101--dc23
                                        2013005127

Contents

Meridians of Thought / 61

Preface

We are constituted to think and reflect, to query and question, to seek answers and not stop at the answers we find, pushing further and further on our quest for meaning and insight into the big and the small, into first things and last. In other words, we are *philosophical* creatures.

How, then, can we achieve more satisfying, rich, creative, and fulfilled lives *as* creatures of thought and reflection, *as* fundamentally *philosophical* beings?

This question lies at the heart of Yoga for the Mind, which came to us in a flash of inspiration after an extended period of reflection and dialogue on how philosophy might be done *differently* – in an embodied, lived, and life-enhancing way – and, concomitantly, on how we might live more philosophically, more attuned to the spiritual, speculative and ethical, dimension of our being.

Beginning from the notion that philosophical thinking is to the mind what yoga (as widely understood) is to the body, we came to adopt the view that the categorical separation of body and mind is essentially untenable (its historical-conceptual staying power notwithstanding) and that, consequently, both *philosophical thinking* and *yoga* pertain to body and mind in an equal – albeit not identical – manner, pointedly captured in the integral notion of *Yoga for the Mind*.

The Yoga for the Mind logo – two overlapping circles containing the likenesses of the Thinker and a woman in Eagle Pose, respectively, both facing each other – articulates this lived interpenetration of our physical and mental being as well as its dialogical matrix.

Written independently, yet guided by the same inspiration, the two parts of *Yoga for the Mind* do not form a linear progression. Rather – as we discovered *after* each part had been completed – they complement each other to form a living whole that can be read in no particular order with the same life-enhancing results.

Both an ethic and a method – a spiritual guide to a mentally and emotionally satisfying life *and* a manual laying out the concrete steps that will take us there – Yoga for the Mind is accessible and speaks to anyone anywhere.

M. E. & K. S.

A New Ethic
for
Thinking and Being

by

Michael Eskin

For what is important is not the particular things to be done but the attitude – the inner feeling and disposition – of the doer.

(Alan Watts)

A mind once stretched ... never regains its original dimension.

(Oliver Wendell Holmes)

Far too rarely do we consider how much freedom it takes to freely utter even the tiniest original thought.

(Walter Benjamin)

We never understand these things until we experience them. We will have to see and feel them ourselves. Simply listening to explanations and theories will not do.

(Swami Vivekananda)

1. Situation

We cannot escape being situated – *situation* being the mode we exist in from our first to our last breath. The sum total of psychological, physical, and historical givens that make up our lives' fluid, ever-changing concrete circumstances – our situation is what shapes and is in turn shaped by us. No sooner do we enter this world than we are threaded into a densely woven fabric of relations, hopes and expectations, freedoms, possibilities and limitations, demands and restrictions, duties and obligations. While being enmeshed with the situations of countless others, each individual life unfolds within the parameters of its own unique circumstances. More or less passively buffeted by our situation's manifold determinant forces at first, we gradually mature into active participants in the continual process of its transformation. As we become responsible agents within the shifting dynamics of our inextricably situated lives, we come to realize that our situation hinges on the core experience of what I summarily call *pressure:* in the face of the human condition as such, in the face of the concrete external circumstances confronting us at any given moment, and in the face of our own needs, desires, dreams, goals, and aspirations.

This threefold pressure to *be, act,* and *do something* at the core of our existence, which both impels and constrains us, manifests itself in different, more or less immediate and palpable, ways – for instance, as the background awareness of the passage of time in general and the concomitant sense that we need to 'get on it'; as a subtle feeling of urgency in the face of the realization that the breadth of our options, choices, and possibilities in life is inversely proportional to our age; as the concrete set of internal and external demands, expectations, and deadlines characterizing any given situation from infancy to old age; as an implicit or explicit sense of what Alan Watts calls "moral urgency" in view of the cultural frameworks (religious, ideological, political) we happen to be emplaced in.

Thus, even the most ostensibly relaxed and pressure-free circumstances will be constitutively permeated by the inexorable undercurrent of pressure at the heart of humanity: the structural pressure exerted by the vise of the beginning and end points of our lives, whose *memento mori* provides the ground bass to the variegated symphony of all our endeavors. Take, for example, the following situation: I am sitting at my bedroom desk on the top floor of the house we rent every year on Cape Cod toward the end of summer, overlooking the magnificent sand flats of First Encounter Beach during low tide, speckled with seagulls recovering from the most recent hurricane; my wife is reading a story to our youngest son; his brother is engrossed in his own book, while our oldest is somewhere out there, taking a late-morning walk in this most serene of landscapes, where presence is all, where substance and accident appear no longer distinguishable, where the I melds with its surroundings, where peace is manifest in the all-enveloping sough of the echoless chamber of an early September day on the beach ... And still, the white noise of finitude resonates through this quiet after the storm, intermingling with the distant roar of the receding surf of Cape Cod Bay. Somewhere in the recesses of my being, I dimly sense the muffled reverberations of the pulsing of time as a kind of irreducible, subconscious awareness expanding in ever-widening circles: that soon our vacation will be over, that certain things will need to be taken care of right after we get back, as I will be flying to Europe twice in the coming month, that I have several important deadlines looming in the not too distant future, that my oldest son has only two months left until his college exams and that he mustn't miss his application deadlines, that I must double check on our family health plan ... that I am forty-four and that I sometimes feel perhaps I ought to have accomplished more in life by now ...

The majority of situations in our lives, however, are obviously nothing like the one just described, which must remain a rare and cherished exception. It is safe to say that the more typical situation we find ourselves in in the course of any given day will be orchestrated to the relentless ticking of the clock and driven by a mix of private and public needs, duties, responsibilities, and exigencies, which we navigate with greater or lesser calm, contentment, and equipoise depending on our personality, circumstances, emotional state, physical and mental health, etcetera. Still, whether we are ostensibly happy or unhappy hamsters in first-class or economy wheels, whether we lead or straggle in the proverbial rat race – none of us will escape the *law of situation*. As G. W. F. Hegel observed, both master and slave are caught up in a dialectic of mutual recognition and interdependence – even the most ostensibly omnipotent being cannot help being under pressure to be, act, and do things a certain way to the extent that it needs others to be acknowledged as such. The ball of being, living, acting, and doing has been irrevocably kicked into our court; from the get-go we ineluctably find ourselves in a continual existential *zugzwang* that we can never seem to be able to live down.

Why is it that our lives transpire by way of an unceasing concatenation of more or less palpably pressure-driven situations, and what does it mean for our everyday lives and interaction with others?

2. Pressure Points

Whatever else it may be ostensibly motivated or triggered by – an impulse, urge or volition, an order, threat or request – the pressure I am here talking about is fundamentally a *function of time*. If time didn't pass, there would be no need or urgency to act or do anything *now* rather than *later*, or at all, for that matter; pressure would loose its grip on us and vanish into thin air. We are constitutively under pressure to be, act, and do something because we are creatures of time, because we live, act, think, and feel *in* time – the matrix and horizon of our existence.

As I suggested earlier, we experience the pressure to be, act, and do something at the heart of our situation in three respects: in relation to the human condition as such, in relation to the concrete external circumstances confronting us at any given moment, and in relation to our own needs, desires, dreams, goals, and aspirations. The reason that we experience pressure in a threefold manner has to do with the fact that our experience of time itself is heterogeneous: for we don't experience TIME, writ large – as a monolithic, all-encompassing entity; rather, our experience of time is more like an infinitely extended braid or helix consisting of three major, densely interwoven strands, which I summarily call *internal time*, *external time*, and *great time*.

By *internal time* I mean the time we *live*, or *are*, as embodied psychosomatic beings – the time of our emotions, feelings, desires, urges, sufferings, etcetera. By *external time* I mean the time in which all else outside us transpires, in which all others live and die; the time created and measured by clocks; the time we all officially live by; the time of history, deadlines, expectations, threats, and laws. By *great time*, finally, I mean the time of our own finitude – that abstract, virtually unfathomable (from each individual's perspective), yet known, truth that we will all die, that all this – the smells, sounds, tastes, voices, faces, experiences, memories that we wake up to every morning – will *one day* be dead and gone *for us*.

This threefold experience of time constitutes the set of *existential pressure points* through which our situation fundamentally affects us: the *pressure point of the self;* the *pressure point of the other;* the *pressure point of finitude.* Because we simultaneously partake of three temporalities – our own, the other's, and our finitude's – we are entangled in a web of interlocking internal and external forces that inform all our physical, emotional, and mental states as well as everything we do and experience.

What this means for our everyday lives and relationships with others is that we constantly have to juggle the demands of at least three masters who not only don't always see eye to eye, but who frequently disagree and operate at cross-purposes. Thus, we may feel as though time were slipping through our fingers and become restless – *metaphysically impatient* – in light of finitude's pressure, while our concrete circumstances and the tasks at hand may demand forbearance, steady persistence, or patient endurance; or we may feel that we have all the time in the world, while those around us are getting impatient with us for being lackadaisical or dilatory; or, again, we may worry and continue pushing ourselves even though we ought to have nothing to worry about and relax, having met this or that expectation, requirement or deadline and fulfilled our obligations. This threefold tension at the heart of the everyday often pushes us into *reacting* rather than *acting* – into fast-paced, shooting-from-the-hip behaviors that stand in the way of a peaceable, creative, productive, and satisfying response to and engagement with whatever state of affairs or problem may require our attention or action in any given situation: impatience leads to rashness, which leads to sloppiness and unclarity in thinking, feeling, and acting, which makes us dissatisfied with ourselves and causes adverse reactions on the part of those around us, which makes us defensive and, soon enough, resentful, hostile, and aggressive, which leads to violence …

This pressure cycle, which we play out in myriad variations in the course of our daily lives, is something we have gotten so used to that we tend to forget that it is neither necessary nor unavoidable. We don't have to become impatient, sloppy in thought, word, and deed, and dissatisfied; we don't have to become defensive, resentful, hostile, and aggressive; and we certainly don't need to become violent. If this pressure cycle is neither necessary nor unavoidable, why do we allow ourselves so easily to be swept up in it? Why do we so often succumb to the manifold pressures impinging on us from within and without? Why do we let these pressures dictate our emotions, thoughts, and behaviors?

Underlying these pragmatically-oriented questions is the much more fundamental question: why are we amenable to pressure in the first place? What is it about us that makes us prone to feel pressure? Why do we get stressed about having to finish something by a certain deadline, or having to act and do certain things a certain way? For, if you think about it, there is no real reason to be pressured even though time and conditions may be pressing indeed. After all, we could also simply do what we have to do, finish what we have to finish *without feeling pressured.*

3. Fear

The first and last answer to the question of pressure is fear. The majority of external and internal pressures we experience are linked to some form and variation of fear. If we didn't fear *consequences* – that the good will end (while we want it to last) and the bad will last (while we want it to end), that pleasure will abate and pain will endure, that if we don't do this we (or another) will suffer that – we would hardly ever feel pressured. We would face any given situation, challenge, task, expectation, or demand *as it is* and freely decide on how and when to act in response to it. *Fear is the medium of pressure as time is the medium of fear.*

By *fear* I mean – in the most general terms – that deep-seated overall sense at the heart of our being that, at bottom, all is uncertain and that at any moment anything can happen that might cause us discomfort or pain, harm or derail us, turn our world upside down (– the unpredictability of unbearable suffering and death being the most extreme manifestation *in our lives* of this uncertainty). It is this fear in all its facets, shades, and gradations – from dread, anxiety, and being scared, to apprehension, nervousness, and concern – that causes us to plan, strive, worry, fret, lie, betray, be submissive, shy, obedient, cowardly, disingenuous, defensive, aggressive, or violent. Fear informs most of our everyday behaviors irrespective of whether we are at the bottom or the top of the totem pole (the white lie being a particularly salient example of the degree to which fear infiltrates even the most trivial circumstances). The most ostensibly powerful among us are as much driven by fear as the most subaltern and disempowered. And while this fear at the heart of our being doesn't always become explicit and isn't always outwardly visible, its subterranean rumblings provide the bass line to the greater part of our existence, reverberating in every decision we make and everything we undertake. *Homo sapiens* is *Homo timens* – the fearing animal.

What distinguishes human fear from the animal's is that in addition to its instinctual component – that crucial survival mechanism – it also contains a self-reflexive, more or less conscious, intentional element that exceeds the immediate.[*] Unlike animals, we don't only experience fear instinctually in the face of more or less immediate, concrete physical danger but also (and probably much more so given the relative empirical infrequency of situations in which our survival is concretely at stake) in the face of more abstract, perceived dangers. Thus, we are afraid of not living up to our own and others' expectations, of making a poor impression on our superiors, of being passed over, of embracing the fullness of life ... For us, fear is not merely a basic mode of existence but also a

[*] In *Looking for Spinoza: Joy, Sorrow, and the Feeling Brain* (2003), Antonio Damasio points out that "most of the living creatures equipped to emote for the sake of their lives have no ... brain equipment ... to think of having such emotions ..."; only humans, Damasio notes, both feel emotions and "also know that [they] feel" them.

basic mode of *interpreting* and *making sense of* the world, predicated on the more or less conscious experience and understanding of time and, more specifically, on our notion and embodied sense of the future. For *all fear is fundamentally fear of the future.* Eliminate the future – eliminate time – and fear disappears in the face of the sheer *what is.*

Clearly, though, eliminating time is impossible. We can only live, think, feel, and act *in time*, which means we are doomed to fear and will, consequently, never be able to extricate ourselves from the chokehold of pressure.

4. Through a Glass, Darkly

I have so far painted a fairly dark picture of our condition: pressure-burdened and ever fearful, we are imprisoned in situations that spawn more pressure and more fear in a never-ending cycle. "Surely, though," you will object, "that's not the case all the time, and certainly not for all of us. If you look around, you will find quite a few people who live active, purposeful, successful, and satisfied lives, unafraid and not hamstrung by any of the alleged pressures you mention. They do not rush to judgment, have no problems with aggression and anger management, and certainly don't get violent in word or deed. And since there are so many obvious exceptions to what you purport to be the rule, your argument simply doesn't hold up to reality."

True as it may be that statistically there will probably be a sufficient number of people who seem to be leading well-tempered lives, act with clarity and conviction, and face life's challenges equably yet with determination, passion, and courage, this doesn't mean that what I have depicted as our fundamental situation is a figment of the imagination. By the same token, it would be naïve to deny that we are all constitutively prone to illness and gradual physical (and mental) deterioration only because at any give point in time there are a good many people around who happen to be healthy and physically and mentally fit. What I am saying about our situation mustn't be understood quantitatively or statistically but, rather, *essentially:* even if, miraculously, you happen to have never in your life consciously felt and submitted to any pressure, or experienced any fear whatsoever, that doesn't mean that both aren't at the core of human existence. Analogously, even if you have never had an accident in all your years as a professional stuntman, or have never had any health issues in spite of a lifetime of smoking, that doesn't mean that, therefore, being a stuntman isn't essentially a dangerous profession, or that smoking isn't essentially detrimental to your health. All theoretical consideration aside, however, for the majority of us it will most likely hold true that we do experience a range of minor and major pressures and fears virtually every day. Just ask yourself how often, lately, you have lived through an entire day without having felt the sting of some variation of pressure and fear – be it in the form of uncertainty, premonition, worry, concern, doubt, anger, or unease.

Pressure and fear foster *reactive* rather than *proactive* behaviors, which are not necessarily conducive to a peaceable, creative, productive, and satisfying engagement with the tasks and problems at hand. Because we frequently *react* to, rather than *act in response* to, our environment and those around us, because, that is, we often don't have or don't take the time, or don't make enough of an effort, to think through and shape our actions vis-à-vis life's challenges freely and creatively, we are prone to live and act without clarity – "through a glass, darkly" – getting impatient, jumping to conclusions, making (unwarranted) assumptions about others and their intentions, becoming sloppy and muddled in thought and feeling, waxing defensive, resentful, aggressive, and sometimes violent, experiencing the world as an ever-looming obstacle we are doomed to run up against.

Clearly, it would be utopian to think that we could ever truly escape this state of affairs, that we could somehow slough off the ostensibly cumbersome and irritating skin of our situation and magically reemerge as unpressured, unafraid, free agents, as Epicurus imagined – if only because we are constitutively embodied beings ever engaged in homeostasis and survival, which means that we are programmed to automatically react to and biologically 'fear' certain stimuli while desiring and gravitating toward others. Thus, even the most ostensibly enlightened and pressure-free among us will instinctually fear anything that might be perceived as a threat to survival, for we are, as Spinoza succinctly put it, made to "persist in our own being."

The question, then, that I would like to pose is whether there is anything we can do about the pressure-fear-complex at the heart of our situation *from within it* – that is, whether we can do anything to mitigate or disable, if temporarily, the mechanics of pressure and fear that determine our daily lives, without disavowing the inescapability of our condition and naïvely aiming for an exceptional state of being and mind – call it presence or enlightenment – that, as history shows, most of us have so far not been able to attain, let alone sustain. After all, the Jesuses, Buddhas,

Socrateses, Mother Teresas, and Dalai Lamas among us have, so far, been few and far between, and there is no reason to believe that this ratio is about to change any time soon. Most of us are more of Peter's and Judas' ilk – fearful, jealous, envious, judgmental opportunists, who tend to overestimate their own moral and intellectual worth while underestimating others', ever ready to point to the mote in another's eye while overlooking the beam in their own. The question is not: how do we empty our minds, become enlightened, and achieve an unlikely state of constant presence, which would by definition eliminate pressure and fear, but, rather, and more modestly: how can we live and act more freely, creatively, productively, and with greater clarity *from within* the inescapable conditions of our situation as it concretely unfolds day-to-day? What can we – as indelibly situated, inexorably emotion-tossed, dependent beings – do day-to-day so as to feel less pressured and afraid, so as to think and act with more clarity, so as to see "face to face" rather than "through a glass, darkly" *here and now*, in the thick of it – immersed as we are in the myriad exigencies and interdependencies of our often hectic and harried everyday lives (at work or at home, with our colleagues or children), and without impossibly endeavoring to take ourselves out of our circumstances? Where and how to begin tempering our fears, reducing the manifold pressures impinging on us?

If, as I have suggested, *fear is the medium of pressure as time is the medium of fear*, then in order to reduce pressure we ought to start by modifying its medium: fear. In order to accomplish that, in turn, we will first need to tackle *its* medium: time. Thus, the very logic of our situation enjoins us to commence by addressing the question of time: eliminate time, and fear disappears in the face of the sheer *what is;* eliminate fear, and pressure dissolves into nothing. Since both conditions are impossible to meet, however, all we can do is work with what we have and from where we are: our situation. Enter Yoga for the Mind.

5. Yoga for the Mind

Certainly, there is no dearth in offerings designed to help us to deal with stress, overcome our fears and inhibitions, boost self-confidence, foster positive thinking, and serve as guides on the path toward a personally more fulfilling and materially more successful life. A quick visit to any of the major book sellers will suffice to make us freeze in view of the sheer abundance of self-help and how-to literature and, most likely, plunge anyone seriously interested in changing any aspect of his or her situation into a prolonged agony of choice. Doctors, psychologists, psychotherapists, sociologists, economists, business professionals, talk show hosts, nutritional counselors, life coaches and spiritual teachers are only a channel, click, or phone call away, should we decide to seek advice or support in our endeavor to live healthier, more balanced and rewarding lives. What more could we possibly want in terms of counseling and professional help? Precisely: nothing. And that's why Yoga for the Mind mustn't be viewed as yet another voice in the choir of prophets of meaning, fulfillment, and wellbeing.

Neither a replacement or substitute for nor an alternative to any of the myriad self- and life-improvement options at our disposal, it is – quite simply – an intensely fruitful and enriching *philosophical supplement* to the daily diet of existence. It never runs out, is free and accessible to anyone anywhere, doesn't require professional approval, guidance, and supervision, or interfere with any other activity, regimen, spiritual diet or endeavor, involves no significant time commitment, has no negative side effects whatsoever, and generates palpable results. Thus, if you ask, "Why should I practice Yoga for the Mind?" – my answer is: why not? After all, wouldn't it be foolish not to do something that can only improve your situation without causing any harm at all and requiring virtually no practical and physical effort?

What, then, is Yoga for the Mind? And how does it allow us to engage the manifold pressures we are exposed to in a way conducive to thinking, feeling, and acting freely, creatively, and with clarity?

• **Yoga for the Mind** is a practice geared toward life in all its variegated concreteness. As such it is both a *method* and an *ethic:* a *way of thinking, doing,* or *going about* (a *technique*), and a *disposition,* a *mode of being in* and *engaging with* the world and others.

• As a matter of *disposition,* **Yoga for the Mind** is literally about *being disposed* – both in mind and in body, in time and in space, internally and externally, spiritually-mentally and vis-à-vis our environment and those around us. It is an *embodied* practice bespeaking our concrete dis*position* and self-*position*ing in concrete everyday circumstances.

• Given that our concrete circumstances necessarily involve concrete others and our relationships with them *here and now,* it follows that **Yoga for the Mind** is an *essentially dialogical,* other-directed practice.

• Predicated on the recognition that we can never take ourselves out of the concrete *here-and-now* and that existence does not acknowledge dry runs, **Yoga for the Mind** is neither a preparatory exercise nor a training for something else to be realized or put into practice later, in the 'real world'. It is part and parcel of the concrete unfolding of life as it happens *here and now.*

• The ultimate goal of **Yoga for the Mind** is to reduce or mitigate pressure and fear, thus allowing us to think, feel, and act with *clarity* in response to whatever life itself puts before us, in response, that is, to any given *problem* we may encounter in any given situation. By *clarity* I mean, following Alan Watts, the disappearance of problems. Clarity implies "transparency, or the sense that the world confronting us is no longer an obstacle," and, as such, allows for greater *precision* in thinking, feeling, and acting in view of the sheer *what is.*

• Insofar as thinking, feeling, and acting with *clarity* means thinking, feeling, and acting in an unobstructed, unhampered, and, hence, unconstrained manner, with *clarity* automatically implies *freely*. Freedom, in turn, goes hand in hand with *creativity*, since it is the essence of the free thought, feeling, and act ever to create the road to be traveled rather than to follow in others' footsteps or fall into a rut. Thus, **Yoga for the Mind** opposes *creativity* to *reactivity*, enjoining us to actively forge our situation – to be *cre-active* rather than *re-active.*

• **Yoga for the Mind** signifies a fundamental *shift in attitude* toward our situation, and, more specifically, it implies assuming and embodying a new, overall *mental posture* – the posture of *cre-activity*. *Cre-activity*, in turn, implies internal spiritual *alignment* and external situational *attunement*.

• The mental posture of *cre-activity* pivots on the internal *alignment* of fourteen *mental poses* – the concrete steps in our endeavor to achieve and maintain internal and external *attunement*, thereby, enabling us to think, feel, and act freely, creatively, productively, and with *clarity* and *precision*. The fourteen *mental poses*, which I further detail in the next section and each of which fleshes out a particular aspect of the **Yoga for the Mind** continuum, are: (0) slow pose, (1) patient pose, (2) stepping-back pose, (3) let-it-be pose, (4) apperception pose, (5) suspension pose, (6) open pose, (7) attention pose, (8) listening pose, (9) seeing pose, (10) in-touch pose, (11) response pose, (12) adventure pose, (13) interest pose, and (14) tuning pose.

Before moving on to a detailed presentation and explanation of the fourteen poses, I would like to stress that, while I cannot imagine that anyone would not want to live a life unfolding under conditions of reduced pressure and fear, not everybody may wish to choose to do Yoga for the Mind to attain this goal. For one, there is no one correct or universally preferred way when it comes to facing life's challenges and solving its problems; in life, typically, more than one road will lead to the desired destination. More-over, some of us might be naturals or otherwise pre-pared when it comes to dealing with pressure and fear, requiring no conscious motivation, technique, meth-od, or ethic to do so. To those of us, however, who have, for one reason or another, hitherto not suc-ceeded in coping with pressure and fear in what one might consider a creative and satisfactory manner, I am offering Yoga for the Mind as a viable method for fostering a disposition that, through internal spiritual alignment and external situational attunement, will be conducive to thinking, feeling, and acting with en-hanced clarity and precision.

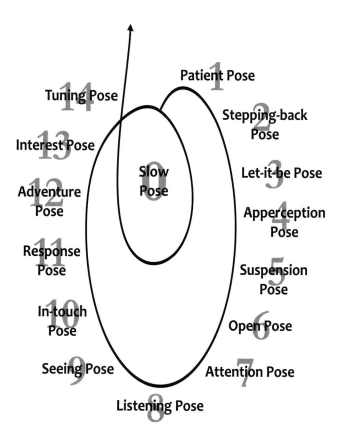

6. The Fourteen Poses

> ... and they also give them the synony-
> mous names of "figures of thought"
> and "positions."
>
> (Sextus Empiricus)

In this section, I lay out and describe the fourteen poses subtending the overall *mental posture* of *cre-activity*, the hallmark of Yoga for the Mind. I should stress that even though, for heuristic purposes only, I present the fourteen poses in a linear, sequential fashion and as a discrete, logically progressing series along the embodied continuum of Yoga for the Mind, it ought to be understood that in real life each pose echoes, implies, overlaps, and is deeply intertwined with all others, and that all poses will be assumed more or less synchronically and in no externally observable, chronological order. Think of it in terms of superimposition rather than linearity: at any given moment in real life, the poses will be superimposed on each other as part of a single, integral movement of thinking and feeling. Thus, Yoga for the Mind is designed as an integral practice based on the continuous and *conscious* – yet not necessarily reflective (once it has become second nature to us) – assumption of all poses in conjunction.

To help us better navigate the intricacies of Yoga for the Mind, here is, once again, the complete roster of its constituent mental poses: (0) slow pose, (1) patient pose, (2) stepping-back pose, (3) let-it-be pose, (4) apperception pose, (5) suspension pose, (6) open pose, (7) attention pose, (8) listening pose, (9) seeing pose, (10) in-touch pose, (11) response pose, (12) adventure pose, (13) interest pose, and (14) tuning pose.

As stated earlier, we are inescapably anchored in our situation. Our situation, in turn, is fundamentally characterized by pressure, which we, as creatures of time, experience through fear. Given that fear is the medium of pressure as time is the medium of fear, and given that we cannot possibly hope to eliminate time, the most we would appear to be capable of is attempting to *slow down* time – or, rather, to *slow ourselves down in time*, thereby carving out a space for ourselves that will *give us time, afford us the time we may need* to survey, think through, and assess our situation and its demands *without feeling pressured*, or at least as pressured as we might otherwise feel. In other words, what we can do is creatively engage the threefold set of pressure points – the pressure point of finitude, the pressure point of the self, and the pressure point of the other – through which our situation impinges on us, such that our very *living time* radically changes pace. Think of it in terms of the cinematic technique known as *bullet time* or *time slicing* (widely popularized by *The Matrix*), whereby the viewer's perception is retarded or distended to such a degree as to allow him not only to experience the progress of any given event in hyper-slow-motion and to notice aspects of reality that would otherwise escape him, or wouldn't be consciously registered in real time – like the flight path of a bullet slowly approaching its target – but, even more importantly, to intervene in that reality creatively and with clarity and precision owing to the fact that he has been given the time and space to do so.

Unfortunately, in real life we don't have the luxury of visual effects to do the job of slowing down (in) time for us. We have to do it ourselves. Which brings us to the most basic of all Yoga for the Mind poses: the Slow Pose.

Slow Pose

The Slow Pose is the root pose of Yoga for the Mind, its ground bass. It sets the tone for and resonates through all other poses. It is designed to shift our *basic attitude* toward our threefold experience of time by slowing us down, setting a new internal pace, stretching the mind, distending our sense of duration, and unhinging the habitual temporal strictures defining our situation. The Slow Pose enables us to recognize that, as playwright Arthur Schnitzler famously put it a century before *The Matrix*, "sheer plenitude, not time, is life – each instant with eternity is rife."*

Like an inner switch, the Slow Pose puts us into a kind of internal *bullet time* mode: however pressing the situation at hand may appear to be – in this newly-created time within time, suddenly, we find there is always enough time not to *feel* rushed or pressured to do anything until we are ready and clear as can be on what it is that we actually need, or may wish, to do.

Because the Slow Pose is more on the *re-active* than the properly *cre-active* side – being primarily a motion of internal resistance, withdrawal, self-gathering, and self-rerooting in more or less direct response to the

---

* "Eternity," Spinoza writes in *Ethics* (1677), cannot be "defined in terms of time or bear any relation to time" (part 5, scholium to proposition 23) – which doesn't mean, though, that it cannot "co-exist with … duration," as Gilles Deleuze and Félix Guattari observe in *What is Philosophy?* (1991).

exigencies of our situation; because its function consists primarily in initiating, grounding, and sustaining a fundamental shift in overall mental posture, in laying the foundations for *cre-activity* without yet properly initiating it; because it is both of the time of *situation* and of the new time of Yoga for the Mind (an existential worm hole of sorts, mutually calibrating both temporal realms), I also refer to it as the Zero Pose: a neutral dispositional fulcrum that allows us to continuously clear and reenter the atmosphere of the fast-paced temporality of everyday life.

The Slow Pose is the first and last stop along the continuum of Yoga for the Mind. It helps us to think slowly while being quick on our feet, and to be quick on our feet in slow motion – which is precisely what Yoga for the Mind is all about: *slow thought for a fast life.*

Patient Pose
{Creating Slow Time}

The Patient Pose is the first proper pose along the Yoga for the Mind continuum and is designed to help us to consciously and intentionally maintain ourselves in an internally distended, stretched mental mode. The Patient Pose first shapes the new temporality we would ground ourselves in and inhabit. It goes beyond simply telling ourselves to be patient, which, as we all know, only works if it is accompanied by a real shift in *attitude* – something that words alone can never accomplish (which doesn't mean, however, that 'be patient' might not be a helpful prompt or mantra for becoming more patient).

The Patient Pose bespeaks such a change in attitude, nudging us to actually *feel* – rather then merely *wanting* or *having the intention to be* – patient by affording us the internal time we may actually need to think through any given problem or situation at hand in sufficient depth. Assuming the Patient Pose, we have already begun lowering the pressure of our impatience by slowly letting some of the air out of the – all too often ready-to-burst – balloon of our quotidian psyche.

Together with the Slow Pose, the Patient Pose forms the backbone of Yoga for the Mind. Together, the Slow and Patient Poses determine the key in which Yoga for the Mind will be practiced by any given person in any given situation depending on the person's basic internal *tuning* in relation to his or her environment. For there are as many ways to slow down and be patient as there are individuals and personalities. Each of us lives and breathes in his own key and according to his own internal time signatures, tempos, rhythms, and moods. Consequently, each of us will practice Yoga for the Mind in his own particular key, style, and pitch, giving it his own idiosyncratic melody, syncopating it according to the unique undulations of his soul.

Stepping-back Pose
{*Creating Space*}

The Stepping-back Pose – second along the Yoga for the Mind continuum – mirrors the Patient Pose in accomplishing in space what the latter does in time: distending, stretching the mind insofar as it is essentially embodied. Enjoining us to take a mental step back from whatever we happen to be immersed in that demands our attention within or without, the Stepping-back Pose affords us a panoramic view of our situated selves, as well as the opportunity to assess any given problem at hand in a more comprehensive and balanced way.

In consciously assuming the Stepping-back Pose, we create a psychosomatic 'breathing space' for ourselves that buffers impinging pressures and enables us to think without feeling constrained or rushed, thus helping us to forestall rash or knee-jerk behaviors. Only after taking this kind of mental step back from the immediate and *putting a distance between us, ourselves*, and our *situation* can we presume to act in a truly *non-reactive* way. Stepping back we gain the freedom required for *cre-activity*.

Stock phrases such as "why don't you step back for a moment" or "let's step back for a moment" suggest that, at one time or another, we have all intuitively assumed the Stepping-back Pose as a way of extricating ourselves from the web of constraints and pressures of the immediate. The key is to *consciously* integrate this, more or less intuitive, practice within the larger continuum of Yoga for the Mind, thereby allowing it to carry maximum effect.

Let-it-be Pose
{*Creating Forbearance*}

Now that these new internal, temporal and spatial, conditions have been established; now that we have mentally created the time and space we need to feel unconstrained and free to think, feel, and act as we may deem most productive, we mustn't omit to translate our newly-acquired internal sense of slowness, patience, and space into a dynamic relationship of *forbearance* in regard to *what is*, on which all that we are and do depends. We mustn't be remiss in *consciously* acknowledging *what is* in its sheer facticity, its sheer being there (without yet attempting to manipulate or act upon it). In other words, we have to *let it be*. For only in *letting it* be will we dispose ourselves peaceably within and without, suffusing *what is* with that sense of lucid and sober acceptance and generosity that is the precondition of any action aiming at truly doing justice – and this means *cre-acting* rather than *re-acting* – to the demands of any given aspect of our situation.

Assuming the Let-it-be Pose, we *consciously* ascertain, acknowledge, and affirm *what is*, thereby ensuring that in responding to our situation we will not be tilting at windmills but, rather, engaging with the *real world*, which, as Ludwig Wittgenstein put it, is "all that is the case."

Apperception Pose
{*Creating Awareness*}

Having staked out our new temporal and spatial parameters, and acknowledged *what is* in general terms, we now need to make sure that we are concretely *aware* of all this – that we are *consciously aware* of ourselves in relation to our environment in this particular situation.

The fourth pose, which I call Apperception Pose with a nod to Immanuel Kant, is designed to accomplish just that: helping us to create and maintain constant awareness of ourselves as dynamically enmeshed with others and our surroundings. It is through the Apperception Pose that we first become aware of our actual *(dis)position* within our situation, that we first *consciously* recognize and acknowledge the *place we are in* at any given point in time.

Suspension Pose
{*Creating Non-Prejudicialness*}

Further deepening the thrust of the Stepping-back and Let-it-be Poses, in particular, the Suspension Pose facilitates a mental stance of *non-prejudicialness* and *non-judgmentality*.

In assuming this pose, we temporarily suspend judgment and allow ourselves, in the words of Marshal B. Rosenberg, to begin "observing without evaluating." It is owing to the Suspension Pose that we stop jumping to conclusions or making (unwarranted) assumptions based on premises that are not necessarily in sync with our situation and that typically bespeak our desire to put the problems at hand behind us as quickly as possible rather than confronting them *creatively* and *with clarity* – that is, rather than patiently acknowledging and taking the time required to adequately think and feel through them before engaging in any kind of external action in word or deed.

Open Pose
{Creating Hospitality}

After mentally positioning ourselves in a non-judg-mental way vis-à-vis ourselves, those around us, and the world at large, we assume the Open Pose as a step toward actively welcoming – opening our mental arms to – our situation just as it is while, at the same time, making ourselves at home in it (even though we may already be poised to change it).

The Open Pose further deepens our disposition of forbearance and acceptance toward *what is* and pro-vides yet another safety lock preventing us from all too easily falling into the *reaction trap*. It is a conscious attempt at acknowledging that everything that is – all states of affairs, all physical, social, and political real-ities, all good and all evil – constitutes an indelible part of *what is*, deserving our full recognition prior to being evaluated or judged, condoned or condemned, adopt-ed or fought. In allowing us to welcome even those aspects of reality that we might be opposed to, the Open Pose safeguards us from becoming trapped in a world created according to our own preexisting ideas, opinions, and values, forcing us ever anew to test them against reality and, if need be, to adjust or change them.

Attention Pose
{*Creating Focus and Horizon*}

The first and most general of the four *horizon-creating poses* – which also include the Listening, Seeing, and In-touch Poses (presented in the next three sections) – the Attention Pose is designed to give us overall mental focus and help us to establish a general *horizon of understanding, engagement*, and *dialogue* within our situation. Like the Apperception Pose, the Attention Pose, too, is about awareness. Unlike the former, however, which puts an emphasis on ourselves in relation to our situation, the Attention Pose helps us to home in on our situation in relation to ourselves. This slight shift in perceptional emphasis is crucial in that it signifies our first concrete object- or other-directed mental gesture along the Yoga for the Mind continuum.

If we think of Poses 1–6 as primarily concerned with getting in position, then the Attention Pose can be viewed as the first pose to *actively gesture outward* from within the thus established mental stance. It allows us to survey our field of perception anew, scope the significant networks formed by its constitutive elements, and reassess what we might want or need to pay particular attention to, how the various details of our situation relate to each other, what our perceived or expected roles within those networks might be, what especially to watch out for, avoid, etcetera.

Listening Pose
{Creating Aural Horizon}

The Listening Pose is the second of the horizon-creating poses. Together with the Seeing and In-touch Poses it forms a sub-set of the Attention Pose. It is geared specifically toward establishing an *aural horizon* under the Attention Pose's umbrella by focusing our attention on the auditory dimension of our situation: the sounds, noises, and words coming our way. It enjoins us, literally, to listen with care to every detail, sound bite, and noise issuing from ourselves and our environment, to tune into our interlocutors' words, emotions, and needs, rather then hearing the perpetual rumblings of our own minds.

Assuming the Listening Pose, we are reminded that *hearing* is not the same as *listening*. We become all ear, our being contracts into a membrane for registering the slightest variation in tone, pitch, timbre, and mood. And as we listen closely to the rumblings, noises, sounds, and words constituting our world, we realize – contrary to a widely-held belief – that, far from implying exclusion, *concentrating* on the detail is the first step toward attending to the whole, that in zeroing in on x we become better at perceiving y and z, that in order to devote ourselves to the *many,* we must first wholeheartedly devote ourselves to the *one.* Like love, true attentiveness – in all its forms and manifestations – is non-exclusive.

Seeing Pose
{*Creating Visual Horizon*}

Third in the cluster of horizon-creating poses, the Seeing Pose is designed to establish a *visual horizon* by directing our attention specifically to what we see and observe both internally and externally. Tying in with the Suspension Pose in particular, the Seeing Pose yet again speaks to the notion of "observing without evaluating," enjoining us to take in as many details within our purview as possible without judging, screening, or filtering.

The Seeing Pose helps us to realize that *looking* does not equal *seeing* and that the latter implies *taking an interest in* and *being with* the world and others rather than merely *being in* or sharing the same space (and time). Assuming the Seeing Pose, we momentarily become all eye, our being contracts into a camera for registering the slightest variation in motion, shape, color, and shade.

As we see, observe, and home in on this or that aspect of the world before us, we are yet again reminded that concentration does not entail exclusion, that in seeing *x* we become better observers of *y*, that, unlike Aylmer in Nathaniel Hawthorne's story "The Birth-Mark," we can be fully engaged with the singular without losing sight of the general.

In-touch Pose
{*Creating Embodiment Horizon*}

The culmination and completion of the subset of horizon-creating poses, the In-touch Pose is geared toward establishing a *total embodiment horizon*, focusing our attention on and putting us in touch with the total, mental and physical, give-and-take between ourselves and our situation, which includes perception on all emotional and sensory levels (visual, auditory, olfactory, gustatory, haptic).

(I should note at this point that depending on the given Yoga for the Mind practitioner's profession, for example, additional horizon-creating poses might have to be introduced under the umbrella of the Attention Pose. Thus, for the food critic and professional chef a Smelling-*cum*-Tasting Pose might be apposite, while the sculptor or luthier might benefit from a discrete Haptic Pose. My emphasis on the Listening and Seeing Poses is due to the fact that they represent the lowest common perceptional denominator among all humans.)

The In-touch Pose allows us to consciously gauge our level of attunement to our situation – the extent and degree to which we are actually *in touch* with what is going on inside and around us. As such, its overall function is twofold: reinforcing our connectedness to ourselves and our situation, and ascertaining that we stay thus connected at all times.

Response Pose
{*Creating Dialogue*}

Expanding the reach of the four horizon-creating poses, the Response Pose is the first pose geared specifically toward getting ourselves into a dialogical frame of mind, toward priming and making ourselves available and ready for actual engagement with the world and others.

Consciously getting in position to respond to the demands of our situation is all the more important given that we cannot possibly avoid having been willy-nilly thrown onto the world's stage, having been always already created actors in the ongoing production of life. It is up to each of us to decide whether we want to play a *passive* or an *active* role in it – whether we want to become true *agents*, actively shaping ourselves and our world, or whether we want to fritter away our existence *passively*, as primarily *re-acting* spectators who witness others doing the shaping and imposing *their* visions on us.

Assuming the Response Pose, we are reminded that *responding* doesn't equal *reacting*, that it involves *creativity* as well as the assumption of *responsibility* for ourselves and our situation, both of which are essential components of freedom. The Response Pose rounds out and streamlines the thrust of the horizon-creating poses in explicitly funneling it outward with a view to initiating dialogue.

Adventure Pose
{*Creating Conditions for Change*}

The Adventure Pose is geared toward allowing us to consciously create the future we would inhabit based on the actions we are about to take. It reminds us that in committing ourselves to *cre-activity* and dialogue we automatically commit ourselves to the risks of the future, to the adventure of the unpredictable and unforeseeable, to not knowing at the beginning where we might wind up at the end – in other words, to the possibility and likelihood of change within and without, which we ourselves harbinger and actively contribute to bringing about through Yoga for the Mind.

The act of engaging the unknown that is the future in assuming the Adventure Pose mirrors and bespeaks a sober recognition of the essential unpredictability of *situation* and, thus, of life itself. It facilitates a disposition of what Gabriel Marcel calls "permeability" – a dynamic state of receptivity, inner elasticity, and openness to the world and others – that is the *sine qua non* of *cre-activity*.

Interest Pose
{*Creating Connection*}

The Interest Pose is geared toward helping us to consciously harness the combined energies of all preceding poses and to channel them forward into our situation and toward our interlocutors.

A bridge-building pose, the Interest Pose both *connects* us with and helps us to maintain the requisite *inner distance* from our world and others (the 'breathing space' opened up through the Stepping-back Pose), without which we wouldn't be able to *let it be*, *suspend judgment*, etcetera. It nudges us to *step forward* and take concrete *interest* in the thoughts, feelings, and needs of those around us and *their* situations while respecting the boundaries separating us.

The Interest Pose takes us to the brink of *cre-action* in enjoining us, for instance, to mentally articulate actual questions for those around us. Assuming the Interest Pose, we make final preparations, as it were, for the dialogue we are about to delve into, the words we are about to say, the actions we are about to take in response to our situation.

Tuning Pose
{Creating Attunement}

The Tuning Pose joins the circle of the Yoga for the Mind continuum *and* opens it up. It is both an internal stepping-off point and a return to the beginning – the portal into the actual future of our dialogue with the world and others, which we have always already begun and been part of, *and* a spiritual return to its own root-edness in the Slow Pose.

The Tuning Pose sums up and bundles the thrust of all previous poses, brings them into internal alignment, fine-tunes them in light of each other and in light of our concrete circumstances, and allows us to regulate and calibrate the *quality* and *feel* of our words and actions to the demands of the given situation without being pressured or rushed. Thus, the Tuning Pose helps us to determine, for instance, when to raise our inner tension and when to relax, when to be persistent and when to lean back or let go, when to fight and compete and when to yield or resign, when to be peaceful and when to use force …

For by no means does Yoga for the Mind imply that we ought to obliterate the gamut of human emotionality and expressivity in the name of complacency, conflict-avoidance, or a bland, hypocritical, pseudo-angelic acceptance of *what is*. Far from it – after all, often enough *what is* must be radically and speedily changed in the name of humanity, freedom, justice, etcetera. What Yoga for the Mind does emphatically aim to accomplish, though, is to enable us to engage *what is* with clarity and precision, as *cre-agents* rather than *re-agents*.

7. Practicing Yoga for the Mind

> … when somebody says to me, "Read me Chrysippus," I blush when I am unable to show him such deeds as match and harmonize with his words.
>
> (Epictetus)

At one time or another, we will all have most likely, consciously or unconsciously, done what one or the other individual pose along the Yoga for the Mind continuum would have us do: we will have slowed down inside, taken a deep breath and told ourselves to be patient, really listened to our interlocutor's words, needs, and feelings, taken a deep interest in this or that aspect of the world, suspended judgment and opened ourselves to the unknown, the other, the future. Moreover, as I have suggested earlier, some of us have a natural tendency to be patient, understanding, good listeners, open to others, in tune with ourselves, and not prone to feeling pressured. Thus, to those who fall into the category of 'naturals', Yoga for the Mind would appear to be redundant, while to others it would appear to present nothing essentially new.

Wherein, then, does the stipulated newness of Yoga for the Mind lie? The novelty of Yoga for the Mind as a method and ethic for thinking and being in the world consists in *habit* or *disposition formation* – in helping us to make those haphazard, unplanned, un-reliable moments of patience, internal slowing down, dialogue, and openness that we all occasionally experience part of a continuous and reliable dispositional pattern, in helping us to translate them into a sustained mental posture that will not only not be at the mercy of the vagaries of mood and circumstance but that will sustain us and keep us on track even in those moments when we might be tempted to fall back on those rut behaviors that we might have precisely decided we wanted to overcome with the help of Yoga for the Mind.

Let me give you a more hands-on analogy to further illustrate this point. Imagine your doctor tells you after your regular annual check-up that it's imperative for your well-being and longevity that you change your eating habits and begin following a particular diet. You might tell your doctor that you do eat healthily on occasion but that you simply love soft drinks, junk food, and Chinese take-out! Your doctor, in turn, might tell you that you should completely cut sugars, trans-fatty acids, and red meat from your diet if you want to prevent the imminent onset of heart disease. What will you do? You have three options at this point: (a) not heeding the doctor's advice and simply going on as usual on the principle that 'we only live once and should enjoy life as best we can while we are here'; (b) taking the doctor's recommendation to heart while only half-heartedly devoting yourself to changing your eating habits (with the likely result that before too long you will slip right back into those culinary patterns that have been at the root of the diagnostic findings that have necessitated your doctor's recommendation in the first place); or (c) seriously listening to your doctor's recommendation and consciously beginning to follow a new, healthy diet.

Clearly, only the third option – consciously going about changing your lifestyle – has a shot at success. In other words, it's all about *consciousness* and *intent*. Thus, while every once in a while even those of us who have a penchant for soft drinks as well as junk, fast, and fatty take-out food will have a wholesome and truly healthy meal, only those of us who make a *conscious* effort to eat healthily will be able to *count on* actually following a healthy diet on a regular basis.

To get back to Yoga for the Mind: like the person consciously committing to a wholesome diet, the practitioner of Yoga for the Mind *consciously* commits to endeavoring to be patient, nonjudgmental, open, and dialogical *at all times* – and not just sometimes – to the point where *conscious* effort turns into *unconscious* habit or disposition.

How to achieve this goal? How to practice Yoga for the Mind concretely, in your daily lives?

Here are four concrete steps that will allow you to integrate Yoga for the Mind into your daily experience:

> • Think through and clearly imagine each pose in terms of its essential significance, feel, and practical impact on yourself, others, and your situation at large. In other words, understand and imagine what it actu-

ally means and feels like to slow down, step back, let it be, apperceive, suspend judgment, open up, be attentive, really listen and see, be in touch, respond (as opposed to react), be adventurous, interested, and, finally, in tune with oneself and one's environment.

• Memorize each mental pose to the point where thinking of the number of any given pose will suffice to set its specific dynamic in motion – to get you into it – and, concomitantly, to call forth the other poses. For, as you may have already realized thinking through and concretely imagining each pose, and as you will palpably notice once you start practicing one or the other pose in concrete real-life situations, it is virtually impossible to assume one pose without at the same time assuming all others.

As I mentioned earlier, all poses hang together – each pose overlaps, ties in with, and implies the others, with which it comes in tow. Thus, you can't consciously be patient without stepping back, letting it be, suspending judgment, opening up, etcetera; similarly, you can't be responsive without listening, being in touch, open to change, etcetera. Whichever pose you may wish to initially assume depending on the immediate demands of any given situation, you will not fail to assume the other poses along the Yoga for the Mind continuum as well.

• Prompt yourself in concrete real-life circumstances to assume the mental posture of Yoga for the Mind as often as possible, to the point where thinking and being along the Yoga for the Mind continuum be-

comes your habit and norm, and prompting superflu-
ous.

• Cast away the ladder of Yoga for the Mind once
you have climbed it. Like a musician who has mastered
the ins and outs of instrumental technique, and can
now wholly and effortlessly devote himself to creating
music without consciously paying attention to technique, so you, too, can now effortlessly live the Yoga
for the Mind way without consciously prompting yourself to assume this or that pose.

It has been said that the proof of the pudding is
in the eating, meaning that if you want to know what
pudding tastes like (and that it tastes good) no amount
of descriptive talk *about* it will ever do; you will simply
have to eat some, and then you'll know. The same applies to Yoga for the Mind. No amount of descriptive
talk about it will tell you what it feels like, or prove to
you that it works. You will simply have to do it – or,
rather: live it – as part of your daily routine to find
out. Enough said. Let the practice begin.

Meridians of Thought

by

Kathrin Stengel

Living without philosophizing is exactly like having one's eyes closed without ever trying to open them.

(René Descartes)

Real inspiration never contradicts reason, but fulfills it.

(Swami Vivekananda)

The ancients did not believe that spirituality made men either righteous or rational, but rather that righteousness and rationality made men spiritual.

(Manly P. Hall)

The human body is the clearest image of the human soul.

(Ludwig Wittgenstein)

1. Slow Thought

Philosophical thinking is slow, and in this very slowness its healing power lies hidden. Just as the one-sided consumption of fast food will cause long-lasting physical damage to the body, so the one-sided consumption of *fast thought* will cause permanent emotional and mental damage. Philosophy is a time-tested intellectual discipline that, so long as it hews to lived life, ought to be an essential component of a Slow Thought diet.

Philosophical thinking is a low frequency therapy for the mind, allowing the oscillating rhythms of thinking to settle into 7.83 Hertz, the so-called Schumann frequency, which is not only essential for sustaining our biosphere but our brain activity as well. When the mind operates at 7.83 Hertz, thinking unfolds on the threshold between rational acuity and intuitive insight, the optimal mental frequency of Slow Thought.[*]

What makes for the slowness of philosophical thinking in particular is that it inherently involves re-

[*] In 1952, German physicist Winfried Schumann mathematically predicted the existence of electromagnetic standing waves within the cavity formed by the earth's surface and the conductive ionosphere. Schumann's prediction was confirmed when, in 1954, he and his colleague Herbert König observed resonances at a fundamental frequency of 7.83 Hertz, which would subsequently be discovered to have a significant, beneficial effect on our body functions.

flection upon thinking itself, which in turn leads to the deferral or total suspension of judgment in favor of the very *process* of thinking. Held in abeyance, judgment is viewed through the intellectual microscope, becoming an object of observation. While the ability to quickly judge and decide may come in handy, and even be necessary for survival, in some life situations, it reveals itself as toxic when it comes to the space of thinking.

In the space where we deliberate and make judgments that entail other judgments *before* we decide on particular actions – the space of thinking – it is beneficial to consciously interrupt the virtually automatic link between thinking and judging. The excessive degree of abstraction that many a philosopher has been accused of has to do above all with this delay, this conscious interruption of the 'chain reaction' of thinking-judging-thinking-judging ... We are so used to progressing directly from thinking to judging that we tend to experience any deferral or suspension of the latter as a kind of pointless running in circles. However, it is precisely this running in circles, this interruption of a reactive linearity that would inexorably lead from thinking to judging, ever moving forward in the belief that on judgment road only advances are to be made – it is precisely this interruption of the ostensible linearity of the stream of reasoning that allows us to recognize its immanent circularity and emancipate ourselves from its automatisms. Thus we become the thinkers, rather than victims, of our thoughts.

2. Philosophical Thinking is Yoga for the Mind

'Yoga' means, among other things, 'yoke' – a joining of two, who pull together and cannot run off in different directions precisely because they are irrevocably bound to each other. The two, in this case, are body and mind, harnessed to the plough of life. The goal is to achieve a perfect concert between body and mind, thereby freeing the soul from all suffering.[*]

In the Western world, yoga is typically equated with *Hatha yoga*. Different body postures – the yoga poses, or *asanas* – contribute to cleansing the mind and keeping *Qi* – life energy – aflow. The poses expand our body's range. Moreover, by gently changing its habitus and opening its often detrimental default postures onto healthier alternatives, they implicitly affect our mind as well. Greater body awareness has a positive effect on our state of mind and our thinking. And since body and mind pull together, Slow Thought in turn – as practiced in Yoga for the Mind – will perforce have a positive effect on body awareness.[†]

---

[*] Swami Vivekananda notes in *Raja Yoga* (1896): "All the orthodox systems of Indian Philosophy have one goal in view, the liberation of the soul through perfection. The method is by Yoga."

[†] Swami Vivekananda's insight that yoga, as a mental activity, will not only change the way we interpret events in our lives but even alter our brain physiology if practiced correctly and rigorously has been confirmed from a Western perspective for instance by Richard Davidson's groundbreaking research.

Yoga – whether practiced through asanas or mental poses – is not a violent act of re-education but, rather, a gentle method of self-realization that enables us to countenance the changes that happen to us only to the extent that they are beneficial in any given situation. The one precondition for the success of yoga is to be sufficiently motivated to go with the flow of the poses and to be aware of these changes. Just as one cannot practice yoga without committing to the process of self-formation, that is, to assuming the poses and following the breathing directions, so one cannot practice philosophical thinking – Yoga for the Mind – without assuming a particular, fundamentally *philosophical* attitude. Because philosophy unfolds in the medium of language, however, it is often difficult to grasp – in an embodied, spatial way – that philosophical thinking implies a basic attitude distinct from the everyday's. There are no 'philosophy pants' – no special philosophical gear – and there are no rituals that mark the beginning and end of philosophical exploration. Just as music needs to be performed in order to come alive for us – reading the score alone will not do – so philosophy, although it may appear accessible through ordinary, spoken or written, language, can only be truly *experienced* by being actively practiced.

Philosophy merely appears to be a subject among others, and that is why any attempt at reducing it to an *object* of thinking is bound to fail. Practicing philosophy *is* thinking, a special kind of thinking that involves particular poses. Like any discipline, philosophy requires a fundamental willingness to commit to the very *method* of treating the subject. There is no one philosophical method in the strict sense, however; philosophical thinking itself is the method. Just as one learns how to make music – its method – by singing or playing an instrument, so one learns philosophical method by actually practicing philosophical thinking. And just as playing an instrument can never be fathomed by listening to music alone, so the joys of practicing philosophical thinking can only be intimated by learning *about* it. Learning *about* philosophy is like browsing through a cookbook. Thinking philosophically, on the other hand, is finding out what philosophy really tastes like. Or, to use another analogy: an art historian will never become an artist by merely engaging *with* art; similarly, merely engaging *with* philosophy without engaging *in* it – that is, without actually thinking philosophically – will not make a philosopher.

When we think philosophically – as opposed to scientifically – the *mode* of our thinking (how we think about any given problem) and the *object* of our thinking (what we think about) interpenetrate in such a way as to modify each other. That is why the lived results of philosophical thinking can never be replicated – which doesn't mean that they cannot be communicated. Experiencing philosophical thinking is essentially experiencing life itself, which is by definition unrepeatable.

3. Meridians of Thought

*Mapping the Pathways
of Thinking*

Meridians of Thought are mental pathways – a map of the functions of thinking, which constitute our existential questions and spring from our irreducible embodiedness and spatial disposition. Just as the spatial arrangement of acupuncture meridians precedes the formation of organs, so the spatial arrangement of Meridians of Thought precedes thinking.

Whereas acupuncture meridians provide an energy map of our psycho-physiological being, Meridians of Thought stake out the landscape of our intellectual being. For a map to be meaningful, however, the principle of representation underlying its creation must first be recognized, only then does it become a map of a particular territory. Recognizing a map as a map also means knowing that the map is not the territory. The map makes a mode of relating to something possible, and this mode of relating gives rise to a new kind of sense.[*] We must always keep in mind that no mode of representing what we are is ever actually what we always already are.

---

[*] As Alfred Korzybski famously put it in 1931: "A map is not the territory it represents, but if correct, it has a similar structure to the territory, which accounts for its usefulness."

Just as every individual body with its features, diseases, and genetic predispositions can be captured in a general anatomical-physiological map and obeys the same universal laws (which allow the physician successfully to perform the same procedure on different bodies), so we all have certain basic mental structures in common – our respective cognitive differences notwithstanding – that are determined by our existential rootedness in a body and in space even before they articulate themselves in speech.* Because thinking is a living process grounded in relational structures (it is thus never merely the sum of its cognitive parts), an interpretive system is called for capable of representing this relational dynamic without arresting its dynamism in its mode of (re)presentation. For thousands of years, the meridian system underlying acupuncture has meaningfully represented the relationality of physical and psychic structures without obliterating their dynamism. Meridians of Thought in turn are meant to provide an equivalent network that will meaningfully disclose the structures underlying our thinking while maintaining their living relational dynamic and anchoring them in our primordially embodied, spatial disposition.

Meridians of Thought are premised on the recognition that our specifically human corporeality has a fundamental impact not only on *what* we think but on the *modes* of our thinking as well. In other words,

---

*Meridians of Thought, then, not only precede Aristotle's and Kant's *categories*, respectively, but condition them.

Meridians of Thought are premised on the notion that, if we were fish or worms endowed with a human brain and human intelligence, we would have evolved, owing to our embodiment as fish or worms, a completely different system of reasoning and would be formulating completely different existential questions. Thus, it must be assumed as a given that our corporeality and, hence, our primordial disposition in space essentially determine our thinking. I should note that in emphasizing this dependence I am less concerned with the basic material conditions of the body that make thinking possible in the first place (our brain, physiology, etcetera) than with the extent to which human corporeality in and of itself calls forth particular structures of thinking that in turn generate particular existential questions. Clearly, our physical state palpably affects our mental capacity: when we are running a fever or are racked by fear, our ability to think is impaired. That is uncontested. The question here, however, is a different one, namely, whether our primordial embodiedness and disposition in space *as such* favor certain structures of thinking over others. Thus, if the body is to assume its rightful place in our system of thought, rehabilitating it as *one topic* among others and merely appending it to an already existing system will not do. What needs to be shown is to what extent our thinking is always already informed by the physical structure of our body, to what extent our corporeality is its very fulcrum.

In a corporeal system of thought it will for instance be axiomatically assumed that my ability to distance myself from myself, to view myself from outside, is rooted in my experience of touch; the experience of being both touching and touched at the same time, of dissociation and unity through touch, reveals itself as the condition of possibility of self-reflection.

If thinking is essentially corporeal – both in terms of its material and structural dependence on the body – then a mode of representation is called for that will adequately capture this structural dependence. The system of Meridians of Thought not only meets this condition but also clarifies to what extent our spatial, embodied being, which is always already in motion, is reflected in the basic, philosophical-existential dimensions of our mind.

4. The Body and the Five Meridians of Thought

Human corporeality implies two-sidedness (right/left, up/down, front/back, now/then, here/there). This polarity in our physical constitution is mirrored in the dichotomous movement of our mind (the one/the other, both/none), and articulates itself in the Meridians of Thought in terms of each Meridian's suspension between two poles, the *yin* and *yang* of thinking.*

Aside from the body's two-sidedness, which is mirrored in the bi-polar disposition of each Meridian of Thought, five additional basic elements or modes of human corporeality that structurally underlie our thinking can be adduced: *gravity; erectness; the ability to touch* (the conscious awareness of touching oneself and others, as well as touching oneself as other); *mobility;* and, finally, *situation* (the fact that we are always already situated, anchored in a particular set of concrete circumstances).

---

* In Chinese philosophy, *yin* and *yang* are the two poles that express the fundamental duality of nature (inside/outside, day/night, light/dark, male/female, summer/winter, etcetera).

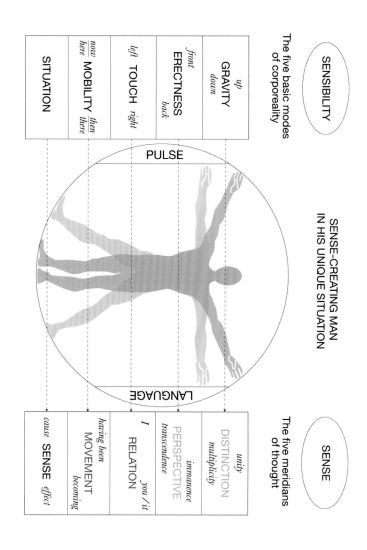

SENSIBILITY

The five basic modes
of corporeality

up GRAVITY *down*		
front ERECTNESS *back*		
left TOUCH *right*		
now MOBILITY *then* / *here* / *there*		
SITUATION		

PULSE

SENSE–CREATING MAN
IN HIS UNIQUE SITUATION

LANGUAGE

SENSE

The five meridians
of thought

unity DISTINCTION *multiplicity*		
immanence PERSPECTIVE *transcendence*		
I RELATION *you / it*		
having been MOVEMENT *becoming*		
cause SENSE *effect*		

The system of Meridians of Thought, which derive from these five basic modes of corporeality and each of which is suspended between two poles that mirror the body's two-sidedness, comprises:

1. **Distinction** – suspended between *unity* and *multiplicity*, and called forth by *gravity*.

2. **Perspective** – suspended between *immanence* and *transcendence*, and called forth by *erectness*.

3. **Relation** – suspended between *I* and *you*, or *it*, and called forth by the *ability to touch.*

4. **Movement** – suspended between *having been* and *becoming*, and called forth by *mobility*.

5. **Sense** – suspended between *cause* and *effect*, and called forth by *situation*.

All five Meridians interlock like gears, depending on and affecting each other in the machinery of thought. As soon as we realize that *gravity* always already anchors us in a *here* surrounded by a palpable multiplicity of *not-here*, we posit a primal **Distinction**. The unspecific *not-here* of this primal distinction becomes a specific *there* through **Perspective** – our orientation toward something – as well as our gradually-rising awareness of the world around us together with the recognition of our *erectness*. Because we are haptic beings, we are always already *touched* and *touching* even before we are born, which means that we always already stand in **Relation**. Our perspective on something turns the unspecific *not-here* into a specific *there* by virtue of our *relating* to it, and we only *relate* to what *touches* us. Transcendence alone is not enough to perceive something as something; we must enter into relation with it. How to enter into relation in turn is something we always already know on a somatic level through touching (ourselves and others) and being touched.

The first and fourth Meridians constitute space and time, the spokes of our wheel of life, for we are anchored in space through *gravity*, and we know time through **Movement**. The axis on which the wheel of life turns is sense-creating man in his unique *situation* (fifth Meridian). Sense is created owing to the relation that we – as *gravity*-anchored, *mobile* beings – never cease viewing ourselves in vis-à-vis ourselves and others, whereby this relation stays ever in motion, and, consequently, sense remains ever in spin. *Language is the pulse* of this relational system, just as our pulse is the language of our somatic system. The pulse of language needs to be understood if we wish to diagnose and dissolve mental blocks, which push the wheel of life off balance.

We distinguish *five* Meridians of Thought: **Distinction**, **Perspective**, **Relation**, **Movement**, and **Sense**. These five form a dynamic system and should be conceived of as the flywheels of thinking, interlocking like gears and keeping the wheel of life spinning. Should one of the five get off balance, then the wheel of life and, hence, we ourselves begin to 'wobble'. Since we are sense-creating beings and since sense often takes the route of language, there must be a means of putting the wheel of life back in balance through language as well. Which brings us to the *Thought Points* situated along the Meridians of Thought and articulating, through language, our essential existential, philosophical spaces of thought. Like acupuncture points, through which our psycho-physical energy system can be affected using acupuncture needles, Thought Points are portals through which our mental energy system can be influenced using *Thought Needles*. Philosophical dialogue reveals through the pulse of language which Thought Points on which Meridians are blocked; and through the application of Thought Needles – pointed philosophical questions – to the congested Thought Points, in turn, mental blocks can be dissolved and thinking put back in balance.

The metaphor of the Thought Needle is inspired by acupuncture on the one hand – insofar as the acupuncture needle, when applied to the right acupuncture point, will dissolve the energy block and allow Qi to flow unobstructedly again; on the other hand, it is meant to remind us that it is by means of the needle that the loose and disjointed can be sewn together, thereby giving rise to a new functional gestalt. Thought Needles, then, can be used not only to stimulate thinking but also to pull a thread through – and thus connect – the disconnected, giving rise to new sense.

In other words, thinking philosophically – practicing Yoga for the Mind – means learning to read language as the pulse of thinking and, hence, to recognize on which Meridian and in which Thought Point a mental block or snarl has occurred. Practicing Yoga for the Mind means learning to diagnose the mental imbalance that pushes the wheel of life off balance. By means of pointed philosophical questions – Thought Needles – the experienced philosopher can help his interlocutor or himself to put the wheel of life back in balance. Even if used only for fun – as a philosophical work-out with or without interlocutors – Thought Needles cannot fail to have a wholesome effect.

Philosophical Sutras serve the practitioner of Yoga for the Mind as memory aids and meditative guides, reminding him of the essence of each Meridian of Thought. *Sutra* means *thread*, and so the philosophical sutras weave themselves as meaningful guides through each Meridian of thought.

Yoga for the Mind can be practiced both by exercising Mental Poses and by applying Thought Needles, which restore balance to the Meridians of Thought. Yoga for the Mind opens our habit-prone, rut-riddled minds onto healthier, alternative modes of thinking and reasoning. Yoga for the Mind may also be successfully practiced simply by trying out various Thought Needles in a playful manner and without knowing too much about or understanding its underlying Meridian system – similarly to the asanas, which work even if we are not initially cognizant of the physiological reach of each pose.

Wishing to present the Meridians of Thought in the most palpable and accessible manner, I have availed myself of an ancient symbol – the *Tetractys* – that has come to be viewed, since it was first developed by Pythagoras, as an apt representation of complex cosmic relationships and their meaningful reflection in human life. Beginning from the Tetractys, I have in turn developed the *Thoughtractys*.

5. The Meridians of Thought
The Thoughtractys

Legend has it that Pythagoras first used the term 'philosopher', and it is his notion of what makes a philosopher that Yoga for the Mind harks back to as a philosophical practice. Following Pythagoras, an essential component of Yoga for the Mind is the expectation that wisdom not only be loved but that it also be loving, whereby wisdom is understood to be love of the beautiful, the cosmos, the union of spirit, form, proportion, and perfect structure. This loving wisdom is a wisdom that implies a particular mode of living, and it should be remembered that in order to be admitted to the Pythagorean School rigorous intellectual and ethical conditions had to be met. The high point of the Pythagorean swearing-in ceremony consisted in taking the oath of the Tetractys, a symbolic figure made up of ten points in an upward triangular formation that was supposed to articulate the totality of cosmic mysteries, from the macrocosm of the universe to the microcosm of man.

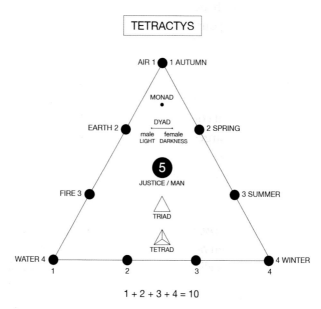

Each of the three sides of this symbolic triangle passes through four points (hence, the name *Tetractys*) arranged around a center point. Traditionally, the number four has not only symbolized the four elements (earth, air, fire, water) and the four seasons but the essential ratios of the universe as well. The number ten, which was considered a perfect and sacred number and which is the basis of the decimal system, constitutes the figure's mystical core – ten being the sum of 1+2+3+4 as well as the total number of points constituting the Tetractys.[*] This sacred number

---

[*] Interestingly, Aristotle's ontology is also based on ten categories, and Moses' tablets feature ten commandments.

is literally in our hands, as is palpably bespoken by the
fact that putting our hands together is the basic gesture of prayer. The Tetractys also prefigures the basic
geometric forms and musical harmonies (point [1],
line [2], plane [3], pyramid [4], circle [5]; the ratios 4:3
[perfect fourth], 3:2 [perfect fifth], and 2:1 [octave]).

The structural composition of the Tetractys – that
symbolically-charged figure of condensed cosmic-
human wisdom consisting of four basic elements plus
a fifth at its center – provides a perfect foil for the representation of the *five* Meridians of Thought, which
build on each other and interlock, keeping the wheel
of life spinning: *one*, distinction, becomes *two* through
perspective; when *two* form a relation, the *third* comes
about; relation is alive, is movement, brings the *fourth*
into play; man, finally – sense-creating – rests in this
living dynamic's center of gravity – man is the *fifth*.
At the center of the wheel-of-life, then, stands man,
anchored by gravity in his unique situation (axis of
space), ever in motion (axis of time). Movement
makes for the axis of time, enabling us to go forward
and backward in our web of relations, while the axis
of space vertically divides the Thoughtractys, thus in-
dicating that in our unique situation we are always
subject to the conditions of space and that owing to
our two-sidedness thinking is always already suspended between two poles. In man sense and sensibility coincide.

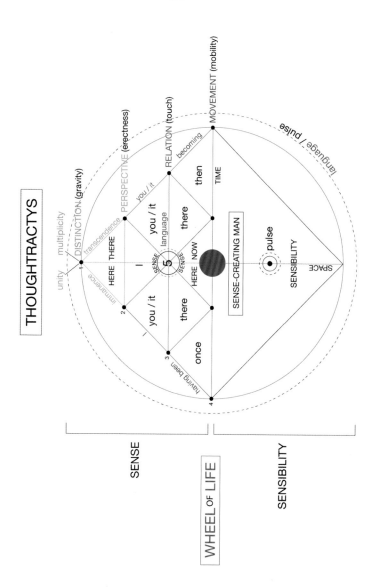

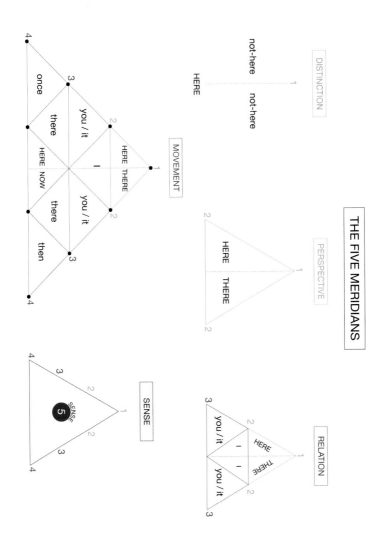

THE FIVE MERIDIANS

DISTINCTION

HERE   not-here

not-here

MOVEMENT

HERE   HERE
        THERE

PERSPECTIVE

HERE

THERE

RELATION

you / it   HERE

you / it   THERE

once   there
        you / it
there   HERE NOW
        you / it
then   there

SENSE

5
SENSE

In what follows, I lay out the Meridians of Thought and sketch their interface.* I provide a list of essential philosophical Thought Points, which may be supplemented by additional Thought Points as part of one's own individual philosophical practice. Finally, I offer a range of exemplary philosophical Thought Needles. Coming up with one's own Thought Needles is one of the goals of Yoga for the Mind and part of the creative process of Slow Thought.

* For the convenience of practitioners of Chinese Five Element Theory, I also indicate how the five Meridians of Thought can be meaningfully correlated with the five elements (and, hence, with the five colors, emotions, seasons, and the corresponding organs/officials). It is my hope that my explanations will facilitate the diagnosis of mental disturbances.

6. The Five Meridians of Thought

First Meridian: Distinction

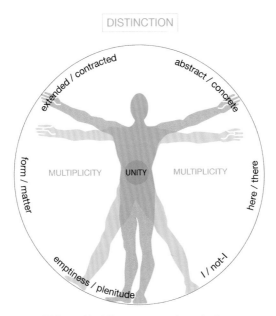

Philosophical Sutra: *you need one for two*

Polarity: *unity/multiplicity**

Philosophical Thought Points:
I/not-I, here/there, abstract/concrete, extended/contracted, form/matter, emptiness/plenitude

---

*Correlation with Chinese Five Element Theory: element: earth; organs/officials: spleen, stomach; emotion: worry, sympathy; season: late summer; color: yellow.

Distinction marks the beginning. We posit ourselves as a unity over against the surrounding multiplicity by introducing a distinction between our internal sense of space and the space surrounding it. Owing to our embodied sense of space, we draw a line between *inside* and *outside*. This primal distinction makes all other distinctions possible. George Spencer-Brown, whose *primary algebra* is based on this primal distinction, has reflected upon it with unparalleled acuity:

> The skin of a living organism cuts off an outside from an inside. So does the circumference of a circle in a plane. By tracing the way we represent such a severance, we can begin to reconstruct, with an accuracy and coverage that appear almost uncanny, the basic forms underlying linguistic, mathematical, physical and biological science, and can begin to see how familiar laws of our own experience follow inexorably from the original act of severance. The act is itself already remembered, even if unconsciously, as our first attempt to distinguish different things in a world where, in the first place, the boundaries can be drawn anywhere we please.

Any relation between knowing and known springs from this primal distinction between *inside* and *outside*, for we can only begin knowing by drawing a line between internal and external space. Barring this delimitation, knowing and known would collapse into each other. For knowing means *identifying, positing something as one*, and this positing of something as something in turn means *distinguishing* it from something else. Although our body's orientation is inherently two-sided (right/left, up/down, front/back), it is nonetheless *felt* as a unity in its very two-sidedness. This *feeling* of unity must not be equated with the *knowledge* of unity, which, unlike the former, hinges on being distinct from another, and thus on a stipulated duality. In the process of differentiation, the *one* is posited as distinct from *all* else.

It is questionable whether unity is *thinkable* at all without implying duality. Perhaps that is why we have to go through the *experience* of meditation, the *experience* of contemplation if we wish to truly *experience* ourselves as a unity, for when we posit or think of ourselves as a unity, the knowledge involved is already based on duality: distinguishing *one* from the *other*. The experience of unity requires letting go of all distinction; it is a *conscious experience* of reversal (which can only be lived, not thought), of undoing the line we have drawn between *inside* and *outside*, the inaugural gesture of the embodied mind. That is why children cannot meaningfully be called 'enlightened', even though they may experience this unity at the beginning of life, for the difficulty of spiritual fulfillment consists precisely in finding our way back to this unity-before-distinction, in *consciously experiencing* the unity we left behind in our cognitive self-quest. This insight is expressed with particular poignancy in First Corinthians: as we leave all childish things behind, we posit a distinction; in our endeavor to know, we begin viewing ourselves as distinct from the world and from our own experiences, and yet it is as if we were viewing ourselves in a blurry, scratched-up mirror; as we become truly knowing, however – capable of consciously reversing this primal distinction – we begin to see "face to face"; knowing and being known, separated by the primal distinction, are reunited in the one who knows "even as also he is known"; the road to this reunion is love; faith and hope will take us to the brink of reunion, but it is love alone that will allow us to see "face to face," freed from reflection's detours and mazes.[*]

At the stage of the primal distinction we somatically experience a *here* and a *there*, an *inside* and an *outside* in the most general sense. And even though our body is the space within which this primal distinction is experienced, it too can become an *outside* if the line between *inside* and *outside* is shifted. Thus, a hurting limb can become something external to us despite being part of – and thus *inside* – our body.

The primal distinction signifies the ability to draw distinctions *as such*, to delimit the *one* from the *other*, which derives from our corporeality and from our awareness that our body is distinct from other bodies and things. As soon as we draw a line between *inside* and *outside*, as soon as we posit a distinction between the *one* and the *other*, we fall out of the primordial ex-

---

[*] "When I was a child, I spake as a child, I understood as a child, I thought as a child: but when I became a man, I put away childish things. For now we see through a glass, darkly; but then face to face: now I know in part; but then shall I know even as also I am known. And now abideth faith, hope, love, these three; but the greatest of these is love" (1 Corinthians 13:11-13).

perience of unity, and space and time are no longer synchronized. What occurs simultaneously in lived experience is cognitively separated in the process of differentiation, which inexorably foregrounds some things while relegating others to the background. Which of the many aspects of the space surrounding us will be foregrounded is determined at the moment the distinction is drawn. In the process of differentiation we first determine the *one*, posit ourselves as sensorial spaces, only then do we assign a place to the *other*.

Because we often equate the *one-as-distinct-from-the-other* with the I, we also equate the primal distinction with the material boundaries set by our senses. Touch, vision, hearing, smell, and taste constitute the natural, physiological circumference of our sensorial space. From now on, everything that occurs within the purview of the senses belongs to the internal space of the I, while everything that impinges on it constitutes the space outside. And it is precisely when the borders of our skin and our senses are equated with the I, and the emergence and passing of these borders are taken to be synonymous with the emergence and passing of the I, that the first, fundamental philosophical questions arise.

Philosophical Thought Needles

What corresponds to the I? Is 'I' a name for my body? What happens to the I when the body passes – does the

I pass as well? What was the I before it became conscious of itself *as* I? How did the distinction between I and not-I arise, if not owing to something that preceded the I and was capable of drawing the primal distinction? How can we ever comprehend a *beyond here* – a *there* – if it is not subject to the same criteria of cognition as the *here*? Does this mean that there is no *there* (idealism/realism)? Or does what we posit as *there* always already determine the space within? Is our internal space of experience – what we sense as *here* – always already dependent on being fed experiences from outside (materialism/empiricism)? Why do we *have* a headache but *are* depressive? In other words, why is my headache – unlike being depressive – not I?[*]

---

[*] Siri Hustvedt draws attention to this distinction in her 2011 book *The Shaking Woman.*

Second Meridian: Perspective

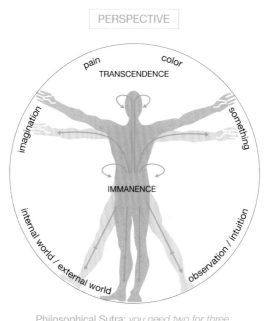

Philosophical Sutra: *you need two for three*

Polarity: *immanence/transcendence**

Philosophical Thought Points: *internal world/external world, observation/intuition, absolute/relative, something, color, pain, imagination, aspect, moment*

---

*Correlation with Chinese Five Element Theory: element: wood; organs/officials: gall bladder, liver; emotion: anger; season: spring; color: green.

The primal distinction is the hub around which our world turns. It hinges on the fact that being subject to the laws of gravity we can only ever be *here* even though we can posit a *there*. We cannot lose ourselves because we are always already where we are; at the same time, however, it is precisely because we are anchored in gravity that the space of perception opens before us in its entire *there*-ness. The space of perception unfolds in our relation to a *there*, to the space outside we have posited, whereby everything we perceive in that space will perforce be subject to our singular perspective – the very notion of which relies on the uniquely posited *here*. Assuming a perspective means determining foreground and background while knowing that the two may shift anytime. Which means that perspective oscillates between the foreground it chooses and the background it sets.

The relation between inside and outside is essentially dynamic, resembling a puzzle picture, which does not allow for the simultaneous perception of its two aspects:

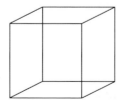

Because our body is anchored by the laws of gravity, inside and outside perspective can never completely coincide. Just as a puzzle picture's two aspects cannot be seen at the same time, so we cannot assume an inside and outside perspective simultaneously. The coincidence of inside and outside could only be experienced at the expense of the primal distinction and, hence, of any possibility of distinguishing between inside and outside perspective.

This does not mean that something inside cannot be experienced as outside. Our foot, for instance, can be perceived as a space of pain from inside, but it can also morph into something outside, into a space that can be anatomically described *as a foot* from which a splinter that presumably causes the pain needs to be removed. Our internal sensation of pain can suddenly shift, such that we are no longer at its mercy, being now able to consider it from the outside perspective of a physician whose analytical gaze only sees *a foot with a splinter* and who is no longer rooted in the *it-hurts-here*.

Similarly to switching perspectives when looking at a puzzle picture, we are capable of transcending our internally posited body awareness, crossing the borders of our skin and viewing ourselves and the world from outside. This act of transcendence, which reverses the narrowing-down that occurs in the primal distinction's emphasis on our corporeal space and its boundaries by mentally surpassing it, enables us to see the *here* as a potential *there*, to remain anchored in the *here* while looking at it from a bird's eye view or from another person's or God's. That is why we are capable of seeing the whole tree even though we can actually only access it from our limited perspective. We are capable of complementing the latter's bounded *here* with as many other *here*-positions as will allow us to experience the tree in all its magnificence.

In other words, perspective allows us to be *here* and *not here* at the same time, which is the precondition for three-dimensionality both physical and psychological. Without this construct we would see the world exclusively from the front and as devoid of depth because we can actually never see it both front and back simultaneously. On the psychological plane, this power of transcendence allows us to empathize with ourselves and others. It is only because we are capable of offsetting one perspective's limitations by assuming another perspective – by changing an inside perspective or by supplementing an outside perspective with another perspective – that the world's spatiality opens before us. From the very beginning, our power of transcendence is anchored in our haptic experience, which continually overcomes the limitations of vision, giving our world not only spatiality but reciprocity as well. Something speaks to us only insofar as we know what it feels like to touch and be touched.

Perspective oscillates between the *one* and the *other*, and in this movement a *third* comes about, the knowledge or idea of *something*. There is a danger that we cease being conscious of this oscillation and start behaving as if the accumulation of different viewpoints could add up to an objective perspective. This would be an illusion, however, as any transcendence of our internal space toward external space, any concrete identification of the externally perceived, is already based on the primal distinction, which delimits our unique *here* from any possible *there*. There is no unadulterated, objective *here*. And even if, owing to advances in the sciences and the development of putatively rigorous criteria of objectivation and generalization, we may have succeeded in virtually eliminating the gravity of any given singular perspective, we can never get rid of residual oscillation. Our inside perspective, as soon as it is recognized as such, will have always already been modified by discursive formation and cultural adaptation, which in turn influences the different perspectives on what we perceive. Hence, there can be no perfect outside perspective. What may appear as subjectively unadulterated, objective knowledge to us will appear to another culture as but a modified inside perspective whose universal validity is anything but given.

Perspective, then, should not be visualized as a kind of 'perceptual beam'; it should not be equated with a geometric line that our eyes project into the world and that returns a miniature, upside-down version of the perceived object to our retina.

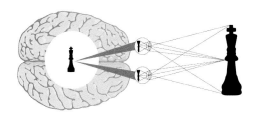

Perspective is the incessant oscillation between what is posited as inside and outside, respectively. It shifts depending on how *here* and *there* shape up. Our own viewpoint as well as the viewpoint of human clusters, which we are always already part of, is subject to gravity. Prior to any valuation, gravity endows our outlook with its very own, unique fulcrum, which engenders our relation to our specific *here*, which in turn allows for relative knowledge at best. Only if we assume God's point of view, only if we move our fulcrum to an imagined outside that is no longer subject to the laws of gravity and corporeality will we achieve an absolute or objective perspective on the world. This absolute or objective vantage point, however, will perforce remain a fiction, for it will either be supra-sensual or sense-less, and thus the result of abstraction.

Losing our corporeal gravity, relinquishing our already assigned *here* in favor of a sanitized, hollow position punctured by imagined outside perspectives means losing the very liveness of perspective. For it is our unique point of view as well as our unobstructed access to it in our very own here-and-now — which means in absolute presence — that anchors us in life and enables us to step outside (without disavowing) ourselves. This applies to individuals and clusters alike — be they religiously, geographically, or culturally motivated. If the *here* becomes heteronomous, finding itself ruled from a permanent bird's eye view on itself, from an imagined position of objectivity, then a uniformity is brought about that only looks like unity without being it in the least. You need *one* for *two*, and the *third* emerges in the movement between the *one* and the *other*, and is gone as soon as this movement freezes. Endeavoring to assume a permanent outside perspective on what we already experience as our singular *here* is like trying to analyze our breath in our own corpse. Breath can only be experienced in breathing, it does not become any more comprehensible when held.

The absolute point of view is one stripped of perspective, one that knows neither *here* nor *there* and sees nothing and all. Pretending to occupy such an imagined place may help us to expand our understanding of our limitations; but it is impossible for us to actually assume this point-without-view in any lived sense. Perhaps we come closest to it whenever we momentarily experience a collapse of *here* and *there* into our point of departure – our primordial, lived pre-primal-distinction unity. The moment when the breath turns, when inbreath tips into outbreath would be comparable to such an experience. This moment of reversal, this tipping point can never be arrested or captured. The absolute is in motion. It is no place one can visit, no parameter one can go by; it is but a moment of reversal in the puzzle picture of experience.

Philosophical Thought Needles

What can be known absolutely and what only relatively? In what way do observation and intuition differ? How do we know that objects are three-dimensional even when we cannot touch them? How do we know that objects are still there when we no longer perceive them? How can we recognize an object as one and the same even though in the dark it looks different from what it looks like at dawn? When does perception end and imagination begin? To what extent is the world of our perception imagined? How do we know what any given thing is? Can we really see color? To what extent is our knowledge of the external world based on what we learn about it from others? Is this knowledge, which is profoundly shaped by others, knowledge about *the world* any longer at all? Can we ever imagine another's pain? What is it that makes one thing resemble another?

Third Meridian: Relation

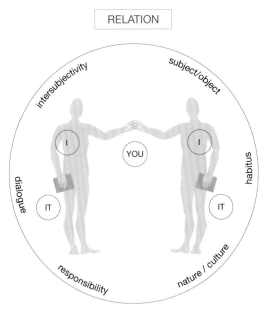

Philosophical Sutra: *you need three to be*

Polarity: *I/you (it)*[*]

Philosophical Thought Points: *body, mind, soul, nature/culture, world, ethos, habitus, power, subject/object, intersubjectivity, dialogue, love, friendship, consensus, sympathy, antipathy, responsibility, person, lust, attention, authenticity, will*

---

[*] Correlation with Chinese Five Element Theory: element: fire; organs/officials: heart, small intestine, heart protector, triple burner; emotion: joy, love, forgiveness; season: summer; color: red.

Space cannot be thought without transcendence, and transcendence cannot be thought without the experience of touch, which continually breaks through the limitations of vision, thereby endowing the world with three-dimensionality and reciprocity. Something can speak to us because we know what it feels like to touch and be touched.

Relation, then, only takes place insofar as *it* touches us, and any perspective on something is only perspective in its relation to that something, which, in turn, is based on allowing ourselves to be touched by all that surrounds us. What does not touch us, what does not concern us has the *potential* to touch us, but it is not part of our world. Inanimate objects within our world touch us differently from animate beings who can reciprocate or reject our touch. Self-perception, too, is rooted in being touched by another. We are part of the other at first, inside him, and only a few months after our birth do we learn to distinguish between ourselves and the other. In our dialogue with the other, and above all through mutual touch, the boundary between *here* and *there* arises, the somatic experience that allows us to draw the primal distinction. At first, the I is simply a *here* that is touched and addressed; much later does it consciously posit itself as the center and limit of this internal space. The recognition that we are not the other and that we are separate from all others fosters our ability to communicate, by means of which we endeavor to bridge the chasm between ourselves and others.

Through touch an exchange between inside and outside takes place, and in this exchange, in this fusion an independent third is created – the relation between the two sides of this oscillation. Relation is the invisible third between two, and always in motion; without it, there can be no future or past. Looking back to the past is one kind of relation, looking ahead to the future is another kind of relation. Being in the here-and-now is relating to relation itself, is *being* relation.

The basic model of all relation is that between *I* and *you* – all other relations are variations of this basic model. Relating to ourselves, we can either be this relation to a unique *here* – in which case we *are* body, mind, and soul all at once – or we can relate to ourselves as a *you* – in which case we regard ourselves as *other*. Our body is externally accessible to us through our mirror image and through self-touch. We can also relate to that which speaks to us but which we don't see, rendering it – as spirit, soul, or emotion – external to our gaze. Invisible though it is, it can be intimated, heard, and felt, and in relating to this *heard*, *felt*, and *intimated*, we externalize what is in fact inside us. Our identity is twofold: on the one hand, we are this experience of our singular *here-and-now*, ever anchored in our being's center of gravity; on the other hand, we can relate to this experience, regard it from the viewpoint of an imagined *there-and-then*, and this outside perspective gives rise to judgment. Judgment is predicated on outside perspective.

Outside perspective leads to insight, inside perspective invites revelation. Outside perspective works through induction and deduction, inside perspective relies on intuition. Depending on how we shift the boundaries, we can view the same phenomenon as inside or outside, which also means that we can assess the same phenomenon through different cognitive modes. Our hand can heal, pray, and caress, or it can be shown, immobilized by carpal tunnel syndrome, to a physician, who will evaluate it in terms of physiology and pathology. At first, the physician might view our hand as no different from any other hand and its pathology; should we start caressing him with it, however, then his inside perspective, which makes him an involuntary recipient of our tenderness, will shift his outside perspective on our hand, and his judgment will most likely change in the process as well.

A judgment can only be made from the fictive viewpoint of a fictive *there*, a potential *then*, or a remembered *once*. The *here-and-now* is a judgment-free space through which thoughts, feelings and experiences merely pass. Judging means taking a step back from living, coming to a momentary standstill, freeze-framing and assessing experience. Judgment unlocks a world full of details that is not at all what it seems. Still, studying these arrested images of reality can be surprisingly useful. Problems begin to arise when the *here* is completely relinquished, when it becomes empty, feeding solely on frozen images supplied from the viewpoint of a fictive *there*. When we give up our center of gravity, we lose our mobility, we stop oscillating between inside and outside, and life – while perfectly explained – remains underfed.

Philosophical Thought Needles

Why do we acquire so many habits, and why are they so difficult to break? Does the exchange of touch already bespeak dialogue? To what extent is self-reflection necessary for communicating with others? How do I form a judgment? How do I know that what I know really corresponds to what the known appears to be? What happens when a subject can no longer, or not yet, be responsible – does it then turn into an object? To what extent has the definition of humankind been reduced to our capacity for speech? Am I the one whom others perceive as a person? How does my person relate to me? What exactly is relation? Can we speak of relation as such, or merely of what enters into or stands in relation to something else? What does it mean to give something or someone power over myself? What constitutes my will, what drives it? What does *being experienced* mean?

Fourth Meridian: Movement

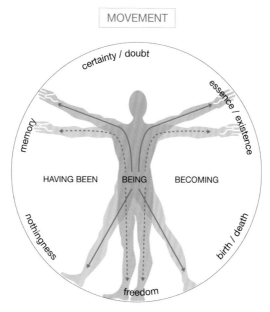

Philosophical Sutra: *you need four to live*

Polarity: *having been / becoming**

Philosophical Thought Points: *birth / death,
essence / existence, beginning / end, constancy / change,
certainty / doubt, emotion, memory, forgetting, man, god,
nothingness, freedom*

---

*Correlation with Chinese Five Element Theory: element: water;
organs / officials: bladder, kidney; emotion: fear, worry; season:
winter; color: black, blue.

Movement is suspended between birth and death. We experience the coming and going of others. We know that all who have come have departed as well, and so we deduce our own end as the corollary of our beginning. Our ability to transcend our singular *here*, to look to the past and the future, is based on our ability to draw a distinction between *here* and *there*, between *now*, *then*, and *once*, even as we are always already anchored in our singular *here*. Although we are irrevocably subject to the gravity of being, we can still transcend it. Transcendence *in space* cannot do without haptic experience. Which bodily experience does transcendence *in time* spring from? We already experience transcendence in time in the rhythms of breathing, even prior to actively pushing it through reflection (contemplation, imagination, remembrance, judgment). As we breathe, we experience the circularity of our existence: coming and going. Breath allows us to witness our cosmic suspension – our dangling between beginning and end, ever depending on what is beyond our control.

Space and time are the elementary components of our transcend-ability, forming the two spokes of the wheel of life. If one of the spokes is bent or too short, the wheel wobbles along, uneven, off balance. Space and time must be perfectly calibrated if the wheel of life is to spin smoothly. *Here* and *there*, *once*, *then*, and *now* must be posited such that the wheel of life is propelled with uniform force. As soon as we think our transcend-ability without its rootedness in the body, as soon as we let thinking catapult us out of our body, we forfeit our fluidity and substitute frozen projections (in both temporal directions: the past and the future) for lived reality. For our understanding, knowledge, and experience it is essential that we do not lose sight of the rootedness of the spatial and temporal dimensions – the fundamental elements in the process of transcendence – in touch and movement, respectively. What is at stake is keeping reflection in flux without losing our anchorage in the *here-and-now*, in *this* body, without forfeiting the gravity of our being.

Philosophical Thought Needles

Does the person we are today have anything to do with the child we once were? Is my essence really a blank, or is there a core, an I that does not change? Is there someone beyond the fluctuations of emotion who generates emotion without being subject to it? Why are emotions so dominant when they are there, even though we know they will pass? If we did not remain the same, if there were no stable core to us, how could we possibly remember anything at all? Do we really remember who and what we once were? How do we access the *once* when we are no longer the ones who experienced it? How can there be *future* for us given that we will no longer be who we are? Our brain is plastic – does this mean that our being is plastic as well and that there is no stable hub inside each individual existence? And if everything is in motion, can we experience movement as movement at all?

Fifth Meridian: Sense

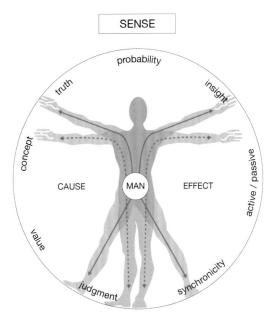

Philosophical Sutra: *you need five for man*

Polarity: *cause/effect*[*]

Philosophical Thought Points: *causality, synchronicity, event, rule, exception, action, effect, active/passive, contemplation, control, insight, revelation, enlightenment, probability, truth, falsity, proof, absurd, concept, representation, opinion, style, definition, expression, logic, example, image, value, judgment*

---

[*]Correlation with Chinese Five Element Theory: element: air, metal; organs/officials: lungs, large intestine; emotion: sadness; season: fall; color: white.

The wheel of life revolves around sense and sensibility. They are the twin indicators of the place each of us happens to be in. The wheel of life rolls along on the spokes of time and space, propelled by the fly-wheels of reflection in their different orbits: beginning from the simple distinction between *here* and *there* man enters into relation with that which touches him, calibrates the living present with the remembered past, is and projects in order to finally endow this entire experience with sense. Yoga is the team of sense and sensibility, and we need to know both horses in order to plough through life and render its span as fertile as possible. Sense and sensibility are the *yin* and *yang* of our being. All sense is rife with sensibility, all sensibility is rife with sense.

Sense often arises through language. A concatenation of sounds, a sequence of marks makes sense, articulates entire worlds. We relate to ourselves and to others, which is expressed in sign systems and structures of movement. Although communication can happen trough vision, sound, touch, and smell, language remains our primary mode of reaching out to others. Language is the pulse of our relational system, just as pulse is the language of our somatic system.

The logic of language is comparable to our body's skeleton: stripped of logic, the system of meaning as a whole will collapse. Just as the skeleton does not come alive without organs, skin, and body functions, so logic alone is meaning- and senseless.

We distinguish five Meridians of Thought, five orbits along which reflection – the Qi of the mind – revolves on the path toward sense. If any one Thought Point along the Meridians of Thought is blocked, reflection gets off balance, which can lead to thought snarls or *rigor mentis*. Language is the pulse we must learn to interpret if we wish to diagnose mental blocks. Yoga for the Mind is an exercise regimen that allows us to dissolve mental blocks and balance the pulse of thinking. Like acupuncture needles or healing hands, Thought Needles must be applied to Thought Points so as to bring any potential hypo- or hyperfunction, which may have pushed thinking off balance, back into balance.

Philosophical Thought Needles

With how great a certainty can an effect be traced to a cause? Is the correlation between cause and effect sufficiently plausible for rules to be established that would allow us to bring about or preclude a desired or undesired effect? What is certainty? How does doubt arise? Aren't the structures of meaning given rise to by events subject to the laws of synchronicity rather than causality?[*] What do we posit as fact? Don't we already need a unique perspective in order to view the factual as factual? What makes a judgment true or false? What is it that makes

[*] In their 1996 book *Synchronicity: Through the Eyes of Science, Myth, and the Trickster*, Allan Combs und Marc Holland aptly define 'synchronicity' as: "Two events, one inner and one outer, connect[ed] not by virtue of one causing the other, but by a mutual reflection of a common meaning."

some facts more noteworthy than others? What are the benefits of generalization? By what do we recognize style? What makes an expression fitting? How do we learn by following the example of others? What makes an image an image of something? How is the value of someone or something determined? What do we gain from knowing the probable? How does thinking relate to judging? What is the role of impulses in our actions? What kind of *clarity* do we mean when we say *we have clarity*, and how does it differ from *knowing*?

Philosophical Glossary

&

Dialogue

As this concluding section's heading suggests, it serves a twofold purpose: elaborating upon and deepening the meanings of some of the key terms used, and placing Yoga for the Mind within a larger historical and conceptual associative continuum by bringing it into dialogue with the thought and writings of others, some of whom may have – consciously or unconsciously – had an impact on our own thinking, and some of whom we simply consider inspiring and productive interlocutors for future conversation, even though we may have come to their work only after developing Yoga for the Mind, or in contexts ostensibly unrelated to it. (Throughout this section, all unidentified translations are our own.)

Adventure

In the 2002 documentary *Derrida*, Jacques Derrida distinguishes between two concepts and experiences of the future – *le futur* and *l'avenir:* a foreseeable, charted, predictable, scheduled future that *will be* "tomorrow, later, or in the next century," and a future beyond this "known future" – the unexpected, unforeseeable, "totally unpredictable" that *is to come.* The latter, on account of its openness and unpredictability, Derrida calls the "true future." The very notion of *adventure* is premised on the notion of *l'avenir.*

Apperception

In *Critique of Pure Reason* (1781), Immanuel Kant defines *apperception* as "consciousness" or "awareness of oneself" (part 1, section 2, §8), or simply "self-consciousness" (part 2, section 1, §16). To the extent that, as Baruch Spinoza suggests in *Ethics* (1677), consciousness or mind can be said to be constituted by the "idea of a particular object as in fact existing" (part 2, proposition 11; see also proposition 13, and part 3, proposition 3) – this being Spinoza's take on the Scholastic concept of *intentionality*, or the mind's object-directedness, and a precursor to Edmund Husserl's phenomenological conception of consciousness as being necessarily "consciousness of something" (*Ideas for a Pure Phenomenology* [1913], §36, §37) – it is indelibly linked to and engaged with the world and others. Thus, self-awareness necessarily implies other-awareness.

Attention

"The [great artist's] direction of attention," Iris Murdoch observes in *On 'God' and 'Good'* (1969), is "outward, away from self which reduces all to a false unity, towards the great surprising variety of the world, and the ability so to direct attention is love." Similarly, in *Altra Ego* (1990), Joseph Brodsky equates the "intensity of attention paid to this or that detail of the universe" with that particular "attitude toward reality" which we call "love." Jacques Derrida, conversely, suggests in *The Gift of Death* (1995) that attending to this or that singularity implies excluding all those who are not attended to: "What binds me to singularities, to this one or that one, rather than that one or this one, remains finally unjustifiable … How would you ever justify the fact that you sacrifice all the cats in the world to the cat that you feed at home every morning for years, whereas other cats die of hunger every instant? Not to mention people?" (translated by David Wills). And Jiddu Krishnamurti writes along the same lines in *Beyond Violence* (1973): "Concentration is a process of exclusion, a process of resistance and therefore a conflict. Have you ever watched your mind when you are trying to concentrate on something? It wanders off and you try to pull it back and so a battle goes on; you want to focus your attention, to concentrate on something, and thought is interested in looking out the window, or in thinking about something else."

Clearly, though, as anybody who has ever truly focused his attention on anything whatsoever knows, concentration in itself can only be said to imply or entail exclusion insofar as it is assumed that we could possibly include *everything* within the purview of our thought and action at the same time in the first place. As it is, however, we could neither feed all cats nor think all thoughts simultaneously. And since, in thought and deed, we must perforce begin somewhere and with a particular someone or something, not giving the latter our full attention would simply mean running the risk of being sloppy and careless in *its* regard and not at all negligent in regard to anything or anybody else. The road to "all the cats in the world" and to "thinking about something else" cannot but lead through the one cat, the one thought here and now. As G. F. W. Hegel observes in *Science of Logic* (1812–1816), far from being mutually exclusive, the singular and the universal, the concrete and the general condition each other. Pertinently, Swami Vivekananda emphasizes in *Raja-Yoga* (1896) that the "more I can concentrate my thought on the matter [at hand] the more light I can throw upon" other matters as well.

Attitude

In *The DNA of Prejudice: On the One and the Many* (2010), Michael Eskin defines attitude as "the expression or measure of the angle at which we engage with the world and others, who, in turn, always present themselves to us at a particular angle." As he further explains, "attitude presupposes a certain level of abstraction from 'pure' immediacy – a certain level of self- and other-awareness that exceeds spontaneous engagement with the world around us." In other words, *attitude* is not something we simply 'have' unreflectively or unconsciously; rather, it is something we must consciously adopt.

The ancient Skeptics, for instance, advocate a specific *skeptical attitude* (*skeptike diathesis*) toward any truth claim about the world (Sextus Empiricus, *Outlines of Pyrrhonism*, book 1, chapter 18). Harking back to the Skeptics, Edmund Husserl, distinguishes between what he calls the *natural attitude* and the *phenomenological attitude* (*Ideas for a Pure Phenomenology* [1913], §§27-32) – the former bespeaking our regular, everyday modes of perceiving and engaging with the world and others, the latter referring to a methodological second-order perspective that we adopt in mentally *stepping back* from our immediate immersion in the here-and-now and focusing on how any given phenomenon *appears* to us.

Clarity

In *This Is It* (1960), Alan Watts describes spiritual or existential clarity as "the disappearance of problems" due to the fact that "the world confronting us is no longer an obstacle." Watt's view echoes the following reflection in Ludwig Wittgenstein's *Tractatus Logico-Philosophicus* (1921): "You notice the solution to the problem of life by the disappearance of the problem. (Isn't this the reason that those among us who, after long periods of doubt, clearly understood the meaning of life could no longer say wherein this very meaning lay?)" (proposition 6.521). And Jiddu Krishnamurti observes in *Beyond Violence* (1973): "Clarity means that you see it for yourself. This is not just verbal clarity, hearing a set of words or ideas; it means that you yourself see very clearly, and therefore without choice ..."

Why "without choice"? Because *what is* – our world in its totality – is ineluctable and has no alternatives; it is, as Wittgenstein tersely puts it at the beginning of the *Tractatus*, nothing more and nothing less than simply "all that is the case." In view of the sheer *what is*, both the common understanding of *problem* as disturbance, interference, or obstacle on an otherwise ostensibly linear trajectory and, concomitantly, the notion that *solving* is what it requires lose their significance. Engaging, going with, creatively responding to *what is* radically differs from endeavoring to fix or make a problem go away. The key is, as Friedrich Nietzsche writes in *Ecce Homo* (1888), to learn not only to "endure what necessarily is … but to love it" ("Why I am so Smart," §10). Love, in turn, is predicated on what Gabriel Marcel calls *Creative Fidelity* (1939) – the active involvement in and shaping of one's situation beginning from the recognition and acceptance of its core truth.

Cre-activity

In chapter thirteen of *Biographia Literaria* (1817), Samuel Taylor Coleridge distinguishes between the mental faculties of fancy and imagination, considering the former but a "mode of memory emancipated from the order of time and space" and concerned only with "fixities and definites," while elevating the latter to the status of a "living power and prime agent of all human perception" that replicates in the "finite mind" the "eternal act of creation in the infinite I AM." Whereas fancy merely rearranges and reorganizes the given – the "fixed and dead" – according to the "law of association," imagination is "essentially vital," it "dissolves, diffuses, dissipates, in order to recreate."

Harking back to Coleridge's emphasis on the vitality of imagination, Gabriel Marcel – author of *The Metaphysical Ideas of Coleridge and Their Connection with the Philosophy of Schelling* (1909) – suggests that true creativity cannot but unfold in terms of *fidelity* to a particular, ineluctable truth – the truth of an insight, event, emotion, cause, or goal – and that true fidelity, in turn, cannot but be creative. This ineluctable truth, Marcel writes in his seminal 1939 essay *Creative Fidelity*, "enjoins me to invent a certain *modus vivendi* which I would otherwise be dispensed from imagining." Following Marcel, Alain Badiou specifies in *Ethics: An Essay on the Consciousness of Evil* (1998) that living in fidelity means "inventing a new mode of being and acting from within [and in accordance with the truth of] one's situation."

Cre-activity bespeaks the life-giving and life-enhancing power of the imagination and resonates with Marcel's and Badiou's articulation of *creativity* and existential *fidelity*, which manifest themselves in real, concrete agency.

Dialogue

As Hans-Georg Gadamer elaborates in *Truth and Method* (1960), true dialogue implies that neither of the two (or more) interlocutors can possibly predict where the conversation will lead and what changes in attitude, thinking, and feeling it might entail. Thus, true dialogue, in which two or more persons talk *to* and *with* – as opposed to *at* – each other, is inherently risk-fraught in that it presupposes the interlocutors' openness to change and the unpredictable and unforeseen in general.

What makes true dialogue so rare and difficult to achieve is the effort required to wade through the morass of what L. P. Yakubinsky calls, in *On Dialogic*

Speech (1923), the mind's *apperceptive mass* – that is, our mental contents at any given point in time, the quagmire of our historically- and conceptually-saturated, desire-ridden, and ego-driven minds, which pulls us back into the depths of its familiar ooze whenever we would heave ourselves onto the dry land of real conversation: "Generally, we may or may not understand what is being said to us; if we understand what is being said, we do so in a certain way, depending on … our mindset … Our reception and understanding of another's speech (and our perception in general) are apperceptional, that is, they are determined not only (and frequently not so much) by our actual momentary stimulation through another's speech, but also by the entire range of our antecedent internal and external experiences and, ultimately, by the entire contents of our psyche at the moment of listening. These mental contents constitute an individual's *apperceptive mass*, which assimilates any external stimulation. Our *apperceptive mass* determines our perception."

Disposition

"Disposition [*diathesis*]," Aristotle explains in *Metaphysics* (1022b), "means arrangement of that which has parts, either in space or in potentiality or in form. It must be a kind of position [*thesis*], as indeed is clear from the word *disposition*" (translated by H. Tredennick). Aristotle further observes that *disposition* can also signify a specific "state [*hexis*] … in virtue of which the thing which is disposed is disposed well or badly, and either independently of or in relation to something else." *Hexis*, in turn – which Hans-Georg Gadamer sums up in *Truth and Method* (1960) as "the formation of a sustained attitude" – informs, via its Latin translation as *habitus*, the concept of habit.

Habit

In *Nicomachean Ethics* (1103a), Aristotle writes: "Virtue being, as we have seen, of two kinds, intellectual and moral [*ethikes*], intellectual virtue is for the most part both produced and increased by instruction, and therefore requires experience and time; whereas moral and ethical [*ethike*] virtue is the product of [custom or] habit [*ethos*], and has indeed derived its name … from that word" (translated by H. Rackham). Thus, according to Aristotle, the founder of the discipline of ethics, the latter is inherently bound up with habit formation.

Mental Pose

In *Outlines of Pyrrhonism* (book 1, chapter 15), Sextus Empiricus' classical account of the doctrines of ancient Skepticism, the older Skeptics – such as Pyrrho of Elis, Timon of Phlius, Arcesilas of Pitane, and Carneades of Cyrene – are credited with developing a set of ten mental *tropoi*, or *figures of thought*, by way of which *epokhe*, or *suspension* of judgment, and, by extension, "quietude in respect to matters of opinion and moderate feeling in respect to things unavoidable" (chapter 12) might be achieved. These ten figures, also called *topoi*, or *positions*, are themselves subordinated to a further set of three master positions, which, in turn, are subordinated to yet another – the "highest kind" of – figure or position – which makes a total of fourteen positions.

The Skeptics' *tropoi* signify aspects under which any given proposition might be viewed such that no commitment to its either being true or false will be required. These aspects include: "contrariety of sense-affection" based on the "variety of animals"; congenital "differences in human beings"; "circumstantial conditions"; and the question of whether the proposition is interpreted in reference to the "subject who judges," the "object judged," or "both." The fourteen mental poses along the Yoga for the Mind continuum bear a surprising – and utterly unintended – numerical and conceptual affinity with the fourteen Skeptical positions.

Method

Adopting George Spencer-Brown's distinction between *description* and *injunction*, one could say that philosophy employs the *method of injunction*: "It may be helpful at this stage to realize," Spencer-Brown observes in *Laws of Form* (1969), "that the primary form of mathematical communication is not description, but injunction. In this respect it is comparable with practical art forms like cookery, in which the taste of a cake, although literally indescribable, can be conveyed to a reader in the form of a set of injunctions called a recipe. Music is a similar art form, the composer does not even attempt to describe the set of sounds he has in mind, much less the set of feelings occasioned through them, but writes down a set of commands which, if they are obeyed by the reader, can result in a reproduction, to the reader, of the composer's original experience."

Mind

As Russian twentieth-century philosopher Mikhail Bakhtin emphasizes throughout his writings, mind is inherently dialogical and polyphonic, constituted by an ever-unfolding, ever-resounding concert of others' words, voices, and viewpoints. Mind is literally engulfed and permeated by others. Thus, any mental activity is essentially other-directed and dialogical – above and beyond Plato's famous definition of thinking as "the dialogue that the soul entertains with itself on any subjects it may be considering" (*Theatetus* 189e; *The Sophist* 263e). Even the soul's dialogue with itself is always already in conversation with others than itself.

Precision

In *The Vocation of Poetry* (2011), Durs Grünbein observes that to "those who take it seriously, who live by it, poetry is a method, a guide to thinking and feeling with precision."

Thinking and, even more so, feeling with precision is also at the heart of Max Scheler's philosophical project. In *The Order of Love* (1916), he writes, echoing Pascal: "There is an *order of the heart*, a *logic of the heart*, a *mathematics of the heart*, which is as rigorous, as objective, as absolute and unbreakable as the propositions and corollaries of deductive reasoning. The word 'heart' … is not the seat of confused states, unclear and indefinite upheavals or forces buffeting man this way or that. It doesn't signify some dumb state or reality of the human I; rather, it is the very epitome of purposive activity … proceeding with utmost precision, exactitude and diligence, and allowing us to perceive a rigorously objective world of facts, which, in fact, happens to be the most objective and foundational of all and which would continue existing even after the demise of *Homo sapiens*, just as the truth of 2+2 = 4 … And in case not only one or the other among us but our entire age should have forgotten this, having grown accustomed to viewing man's emotional life as a dumb, *subjective* reality, utterly meaningless in terms of objective necessity, devoid of purpose and direction, then this is not nature's but our own and our age's fault – characterized as it is by a general sloppiness in matters of emotion, love and hate, by a lack of seriousness regarding the depth of things and life in general …"

Pressure Points

A pressure point is a delimited, vital area on the body whose external manipulation will generate significant physiological effects, such as discomfort, pain or pleasure. Similar areas, which are functionally dependent on situation, exist on the emotional, spiritual, and intellectual planes.

Problem

A problem – deriving from the Greek *problema* – means, literally, something that has been put or thrown before us physically or mentally, creating an obstacle or hindrance – a road or mental block – on our way toward a destination or goal.

Situation

Situation ought to be understood less as a state than as a continual process along the lines of such process-nouns as *promotion*, *relocation*, *expatriation*, *elimination*, *mystification*, or *obfuscation*. Thus, it doesn't describe where we are so much as what we are continually involved in. Among the philosophers who have reflected upon *situation*, Martin Heidegger's and Jean-Paul Sartre's approaches to it as a central existential category inherently tied up with the question of agency are particularly noteworthy. Heidegger defines it in *Being and Time* (1927; §60) as "what, in the light of our decisiveness, reveals itself as lying before us, this being our very mode of existence"; and Sartre conceives of it in *Being and Nothingness* (1943; part 4, chapter 1, section 2) as "the contingency of liberty amidst the plenitude of the world … as already illuminated by the ends which liberty chooses."

Suspension (of judgment)

In classical Skepticism, *suspension of judgment* (*epokhe*) is the method by which "quietude in respect to matters of opinion and moderate feeling in respect to things unavoidable" may be achieved. *Epokhe* subsequently becomes the methodological fulcrum of phenomenology, a school of philosophy founded at the beginning of the twentieth century by Edmund Husserl (see especially *Ideas for a Pure Phenomenology* [1913], §32).

Time

Mindful of Aristotle's definition of time as "the calculable measure or dimension of motion with respect to before-and-afterness" unfolding through an unceasing concatenation of "now's" (*Physics* [219b–220a, translated by P. H. Wicksteed and F. M. Cornford]), St. Augustine asks in *Confessions* (book 11; translated by H. Chadwick): "What is time? Who can explain this easily and briefly? Who can comprehend this even in thought so as to articulate the answer in words? Yet what do we speak of, in our familiar everyday conversation, more than of time? We surely know what we mean when we speak of it. We also know what is meant when we hear someone else talking about it. What then is time? Provided that no one asks me I know. If I want to explain it to an inquirer, I do not know. But I confidently affirm myself to know that if nothing passes away, there is no past time, and if nothing arrives, there is no future time, and if nothing existed, there would be no present time."

Further on, in answer to his initial question, St. Augustine writes: "What is by now evident and clear is that neither future nor past exists, and it is inexact language to speak of three times – past, present, and future. Perhaps it would be exact to say: there are three times, a present of things past, a present of things present, and a present of things to come. In the soul there are these three aspects of time, and I do not see them anywhere else. The present considering the past is memory, the present considering the present is immediate awareness, the present considering the future is expectation."

Turning his attention to the origin of time, St. Augustine muses: "When time is measured, where does it come from, by what route does it pass, and where does it go? It must come out of the future, pass by the present, and go into the past; so it comes from what as yet does not exist, passes through that which lacks extension, and goes into that which is now non-existent."

St. Augustine's pioneering reflections on the phenomenon and experience of time are subsequently picked up and developed by Edmund Husserl and Martin Heidegger, in particular. In *Lectures on the Phenomenology of Internal Time Consciousness* (1928), Husserl re-conceptualizes Augustine's insights into our experience of the time in terms of what he calls *retentions* and *protentions*. We become aware of the passage of time, according to Husserl, in *retaining* (§9) what goes by in what is commonly called memory (§11), and in *protaining* what is about to arrive and pass through the ever-fluid portal of the now en route to the past in what is commonly called *expectation* (§14, §16).

Applying Husserl's Augustine-inspired analyses of time consciousness to the human condition as such,

Heidegger writes in *Being and Time* (1927): "The past is born of the future; in the process, the future-to-be past releases the present from within itself. This integral phenomenon of the future-becoming-past-and-bearing-the-present we call temporality" (§65), which conditions, and is not to be confused with, 'official', measurable, or what Heidegger calls *vulgar time* (§78ff.).

Touch

"My body," Maurice Merleau-Ponty writes in *Phenomenology of Perception* (1945), "is recognized by its power to give me 'double sensations': when I touch my right hand with my left, my right hand, as an object, has the strange property of being able to feel too. We have just seen that the two hands are never simultaneously in the relationship of touched and touching to each other. When I press my two hands together, it is not a matter of two sensations felt together as one perceives two objects placed side by side, but of an ambiguous set-up in which both hands can alternate the rôles of 'touching' and being 'touched'. What was meant by talking about 'double sensations' is that, in passing from one rôle to the other, I can identify the hand touched as the same one which will in a moment be touching" (translated by Colin Smith).

What Is – Now

In *Physics* (219b), Aristotle endeavors to capture the complex character of "now": "And as motion is a continuous flux, so is time; but at any given moment time is the same everywhere, for the 'now' itself is identical in its essence, but the relations into which it enters differ in different connections, and it is the 'now' that marks off time as before and after. But this 'now', which is identical everywhere, itself retains its identity in one sense, but does not in another; for inasmuch as the point in the flux of time which it marks is changing (and so to mark it is its essential function) the 'now' too differs perpetually, but inasmuch as at every moment it is performing its essential function of dividing the past and the future it retains its identity" (translated by P. H. Wicksteed and F. M. Cornford). So, too, does *what is* remain essentially the same and differ contextually, in its very identity.

Yoga

Elaborating on the root meaning of *yoga* ('yoke', 'yoke together', 'unite', 'harness'), Swami Vivekananda offers a concise and comprehensive explication of its traditional significance and pursuit in "The Ideal of a Universal Religion," a lecture delivered in New York in January in 1896 (cited in *The Yogas and Other Works* [1953]): "Would to God that all men were so constituted that in their minds all these elements – of philosophy, mysticism, emotion, and work – were equally present in full! That is the ideal, my ideal of a perfect man. Everyone who has only one or two of these elements I consider partial and one-sided. This world is almost full of such one-sided men, who possess knowledge of that one road only in which they move, and to whom anything else is dangerous and horrible. To become harmoniously balanced in all these four directions is my ideal of religion. And this ideal is attained by what we in India call *yoga* – union. To the worker, it is union between himself and the whole of humanity; to the mystic, union between his lower self and Higher Self; to the lover, union between himself and the God of Love; and to the philosopher, the unity of all existence. That is what is meant by yoga. This is a Sanskrit term, and these four divisions of yoga have, in Sanskrit, different names. The man who seeks after this kind of union is called a *yogi*. The worker is called a *karma-yogi*. He who seeks union through love is called a *bhakti-yogi*. He who seeks it through mysticism is called a *raja-yogi*. And he who seeks it through philosophy is called a *jnana-yogi*. So this word *yogi* comprises them all."

Alan Watts, too, offers a helpful summary of the meaning and varieties of yoga in his posthumously published lecture "Intellectual Yoga" (cited in *Om: Creative Mediations* [1980]): "The word *yoga*, as you may know, is the same as the English word yoke and the Latin word *jungare* ('join'). When Jesus said, 'My yoke is easy', he was also saying, 'My *yoga* is easy'. *Yoga* describes the state that is the opposite of what our psychologists call alienation, the feeling of separateness, of being cut off from being … There are certain principle forms of yoga with which most people are familiar. Hatha-yoga is a psychophysical exercise system … Then there is bhakti-yoga; *bhakti* means devotion.

I suppose you might say that Christianity is a form of bhakti-yoga … Then there is karma-yoga. *Karma* means action – and incidentally, that is all it means … Karma-yoga is the way of action, of using your everyday life, your trade, or an athletic discipline … as your way of yoga … Raja-yoga, the *royal* yoga that is sometimes called *kundalini-yoga*, involves very complicated psychic exercises having to do with awakening the serpent power that is supposed to lie at the base of one's spiritual spine … There are several other yogas [including *Kriya yoga*, which, according to Pramahansa Yogananda's *Autobiography of a Yogi* (1946), goes back to "Pantanjali and Christ, and to St. John and St. Paul"], then finally there is mantra-yoga. Mantra-yoga is the practice through chanting or humming, either loud or silently, certain sounds which become supports for contemplation, or what in Sanskrit is called dhyana. Dhyana is the state in which one is clearly awake and aware of the world as it is, as distinct from the world as it is described … There is an intellectual way to get at this kind of understanding; jnana-yoga is the approach to that which is intellectual…"

Incidentally, it is worth remembering that according to Svatmarama's *Hathapradipika*, our principle written source on *Hatha yoga*, the latter forms an indissoluble unity with *Raja yoga*, both being the two sides – bodily and mental, respectively – "of one and the same discipline called Yoga."

What is also yoked together, united, or harnessed, in yoga, finally, as Svatmarama points out in *Hathapradipika*, are "the mind and the energy of the living being" more generally, that is, "one's [overall] faculties" in mind and body (cf. also *The Encyclopedia of Philosophy*, vol. 8).

About the Authors

MICHAEL ESKIN was educated at Concordia College, the University of Munich and Rutgers University. A former fellow of Sidney Sussex College, Cambridge, he has taught at the University of Cambridge and at Columbia University. He has given workshops, lectured and published widely on literary, philosophical, ethical and cultural subjects, including: *Ethics and Dialogue in the Works of Levinas, Bakhtin, Mandel'shtam, and Celan*; *Poetic Affairs – Celan, Grünbein, Brodsky*; *17 Prejudices That We Germans Hold Against America and Americans and That Can't Quite Be True* (published in German under the pseudonym 'Misha Waiman'); *Philosophical Fragments of a Contemporary Life* (under the pseudonym 'Julien David'); and *The DNA of Prejudice – On the One and the Many* (winner of the 2010 Next Generation Indie Book Award for Social Change). A frequent guest on radio programs throughout the US, Michael Eskin lives in New York City and is the co-founder of Upper West Side Philosophers, Inc.

KATHRIN STENGEL was educated at the Universities of Leuven (Belgium), Munich, and Konstanz (Germany) and has taught philosophy at Seattle University and the Rhode Island School of Design. She has published widely on ethics, aesthetics, and epistemology, including *The Subject as Threshold: A Comparative Study on Ludwig Wittgenstein's Philosophy of*

Language and Maurice Merleau-Ponty's Philosophy of Perception. Her book *November Rose: A Speech on Death* – a philosophical meditation on loss, grief, and survival – won a 2008 Independent Publisher Book Award. Kathrin Stengel has been a frequent guest on radio programs throughout the US and Europe, and has designed and organized international philosophical events on such topics as 'space', 'imagination', 'style', 'pain', and 'color'. For many years, she has also taught Vipassana Meditation and practiced Jin Shin Jyutsu. She lives in New York City and is the cofounder of Upper West Side Philosophers, Inc.

Also available from UWSP

- *November Rose: A Speech on Death* by Kathrin Stengel
  (2008 Independent Publisher Book Award)

- *November-Rose: Eine Rede über den Tod* by Kathrin Stengel

- *Philosophical Fragments of a Contemporary Life* by Julien David

- *17 Vorurteile, die wir Deutschen gegen Amerika und die Amerikaner
  haben und die so nicht ganz stimmen können* by Misha Waiman

- *The DNA of Prejudice: On the One and the Many* by Michael Eskin
  (2010 Next Generation Indie Book Award for Social Change)

- *Descartes' Devil: Three Meditations* by Durs Grünbein

- *Fatal Numbers: Why Count on Chance* by Hans Magnus Enzensberger

- *The Vocation of Poetry* by Durs Grünbein
  (2011 Independent Publisher Book Award)

- *The Waiting Game: An Essay on the Gift of Time* by Andrea Köhler

- *Mortal Diamond: Poems* by Durs Grünbein

- *A Moment More Sublime: A Novel* by Stephen Grant

- *Potentially Harmless: A Philosopher's Manhattan* by Kathrin Stengel

- *Health Is in Your Hands: Jin Shin Jyutsu – Practicing the Art of
  Self-Healing* by Waltraud Riegger-Krause

- *High on Low: Harnessing the Power of Unhappiness*
  by Wolfgang Schmid

- *The Wisdom of Parenthood: An Essay* by Michael Eskin

Typesetting and design: Michael Eskin
Printed by KS Printing, Shanghai